S

Quincy Jones

RAYMOND HORRICKS *,1933-*

Selected Discography
by Tony Middleton

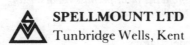
SPELLMOUNT LTD
Tunbridge Wells, Kent

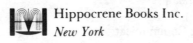
Hippocrene Books Inc.
New York

FOR SHEILA ROSSINI
– in appreciation

In the same series of biographies on popular musicians:-
James Galway
John Williams

First published in the UK in 1985 by
SPELLMOUNT LTD
12 Dene Way, Speldhurst,
Tunbridge Wells, Kent TN3 ONX
ISBN 0-946771-02-2 (UK)
Copyright © Raymond Horricks 1985

British Library Cataloguing Data
Horricks, Raymond
    Quincy Jones.—(Popular musicians; 2)
    1. Jones, Quincy   2. Jazz musicians—United
    States—Biography
    I. Title   II. Middleton, Tony   III. Series
    785.42'092'4   ML419.J/

First published in the USA in 1985 by
Hippocrene Books Inc.
171 Madison Avenue,
New York, NY 10016
ISBN 0-87052-215-9 (USA)

Series editor: David Burnett James
Cover design: Trixie Selwyn
Book design: Susan Ryall
Typesetting by Concept Communications
Printed in Great Britain by
The Moxon Press Ltd.,
Gillroyd Mills, Wide Lane,
Morley, Leeds.

CONTENTS

List of Illustrations   5

Chapter 1   Renaissance Man   7

Chapter 2   Morning Light   11

Chapter 3   Europe   17

Chapter 4   Dizzy For The World   30

Chapter 5   Metamorphosis . . . And The Birth of A Band   42

Chapter 6   Mister Green Steps In   52

Chapter 7   Inside Celluloid City   59

Chapter 8   Smackwater Jack   69

Chapter 9   Affairs Of The Head   77

Chapter 10   Aftermath   83

Chapter 11   Off Graffitti, The Bright Newcomers, Of Ghosties
             And Ghoulies – And Ol' Blue Eyes Is Back, Again   93

A Coda For Quincy Jones   103

Appendix: Quincy Jones – Credits   104

Author's Acknowledgements   107

We Are The World . . .   108

Select Discography by Tony Middleton   111

LIST OF ILLUSTRATIONS

Quincy Jones aged 20. *Melody Maker*

Ray Charles. *Melody Maker*

Lionel Hampton. *JVC*

'This is how I feel about Jazz'. *ABC-Paramount*

Billy Eckstine. *Melody Maker*

Frank Sinatra and Count Basie. *Reprise Records*

Quincy Jones. *A & M Records*

'In Cold Blood'. *RCA*

'Smackwater Jack'. *A & M Records*

Patti Austin. *WEA Records*

James Ingram. *WEA Records*

Quincy Jones with Michael Jackson and Steven Spielberg. *Michael Jackson, Body and Soul* by Geoff Brown (Virgin Books)

Quincy Jones. *A & M Records*

Quincy Jones. *Ebony*

Quincy Jones. *A & M Records*

ERRATA
Due to an error the caption shown on List of Illustrations and on page 3 of the Art section should read:
Frank Sinatra and Duke Ellington. *Reprise Records*

'A clever man will know how to range his interests, and will pursue each according to its merits.'   – LA ROCHEFOUCAULD (*Maximes, 1665*)

Chapter 1

RENAISSANCE MAN

Henry David Thoreau once said that, because Man normally falls far short of his aims, therefore he should aim very high in the first place.

I first became aware of Quincy Jones back in 1953 when I read in *The Melody Maker* that a musician of that name had passed through Heathrow Airport en route for New York after touring Europe with the Lionel Hampton band. *The Melody Maker* article (by Mike Nevard) was largely concerned with another composer/arranger, Gigi Gryce; but Quincy's christian name was different enough to stick with me. Then, the following year, the recorded results of his weeks in Europe began to come on to the market via the Vogue and Esquire labels. I was young too, impressionable, and collecting experiences. At the same time though, I grew convinced that here was a major new talent: as fresh and exciting as anyone I had heard since the first impact of Charlie Parker.

I managed to find an address for Quincy Jones and wrote to him in New York City. Not exactly a 'fan' letter, more one in which I sought to learn about him and what his future plans were. Not only did he respond but our first exchange of letters ripened into a regular correspondence. It was as if, between making music, he welcomed the opportunity to express his thoughts, feelings and, above all, his hopes for the determining power of his own creativity. Later this would bring about meetings between us, interviews and a sizeable box-file devoted to his life and work, on which I have drawn for this book.

What I could not possibly foresee in those days was just how far his career could go; nor how diverse it would become. It simply seemed to me that whatever he attempted was bound to be fascinating. And so it has turned out. I remain as dedicated a Quincy Jones listener and watcher as ever.

His versatility has to be explained. The phenomenon of any jazz artist,

7

whether instrumentalist or composer/arranger, going on to become a huge success in the wider field of popular music, or 'pop', is not entirely new; but it is still sufficiently rare to focus our attention more sharply and arouse our curiosity over how and why such success came about. What does seem plain, though, is that it nearly always happens when the person involved makes a conscious effort towards a shift of emphasis in his or her musical creativity. Outside observers are then likely to experience surprise, or even shock. Not so the author of the change.

One other point should be added. Life presents each of us with certain challenges, which come before us at differing intervals. Some people may call them 'fortuitous', or 'good luck' or just 'being in the right place at the right time'. But these challenges still have to be grasped; and this is a dilemma for the artist, who must believe in what he or she feels by instinctive reaction to be possible, and in consequence stretches out for the opportunities on offer with all his reserves of courage. The arts are heavy with practitioners who age, grow increasingly bitter and spend their days, not merely bemoaning fate or neglect, but declaring repeatedly, 'If only I'd done this or that when there was the chance. . .'

Louis Armstrong offers a specific example of such a 'sea-change'. The first great virtuoso soloist of jazz, he began from the 1930s to supplement his trumpet-playing with warm, gravelly-sounding vocals plus a form of wordless singing that came to be called 'scat'. He also began to introduce comedy into his stage act. These changes gave him lift-off as an altogether different type of popular entertainer, took him into films (*Pennies From Heaven, High Society*) and on to soaring, chart-topping 'hit' singles such as *Hello Dolly* in 1964 and *What A Wonderful World* in 1968. Meanwhile, the gifted pianist and trio leader Nat 'King' Cole (he won the 'Esquire' Gold Award for jazz piano in 1946) had by the 1950s relegated his keyboard to the background and become a very articulate, professional but essentially heart-throb type of crooner. Again a long list of worldwide hit records followed. Other famous popular vocalists started singing with big bands of the Swing era: Ella Fitzgerald (with Chick Webb), Peggy Lee (Benny Goodman) and Sarah Vaughan (Earl Hines, Billy Eckstine), while during his last years Count Basie used his magnificent orchestra to accompany such show-business giants as Frank Sinatra and Tony Bennett.

A further refinement dates from 13 February, 1962 when Stan Getz, arguably the most brilliant white tenor-saxophone soloist of jazz, joined the guitarist Charlie Byrd at All Souls Unitarian Church in Washington, DC to record an album which included *Desafinado (Slightly Out Of Tune)* and *Samba De Una Nota So (One Note Samba)*. Here Getz's improvisations remain rooted in jazz, but they are aligned (skilfully) with some commercial-sounding Latin American rhythms — and the discs swept the nation and all other continents as the *bossa nova* craze. A year later Getz recorded *The Girl From Ipanema* with Astrud, wife of the Brazilian composer Joao Gilberto. It proved another blockbuster in the popular music charts.

Nor does the process end with this. It can be said also that Miles Davis, edging into a jazz-rock fusion by the 1970s, is another example of boundary breaking, away from modern jazz proper; similarly, the group Weather Report, and the English guitarist John McLaughlin forming the Mahavishnu Orchestra and making records with the outstanding pop guitarist Carlos Santana.

But here we reach controversy. Early mutterings of 'betrayal', 'a sell-out' or 'exchanging one's birthright for a mess of pottage' have grown into a vociferous cacophony of abuse against such moves. Jazz purists (including many reviewers) vary in their condemnations, but condemn they do, and strongly. Louis Armstrong's clowning has been dubbed 'Uncle Tom', his hit-singles as a mere scrabble for gold; Nat Cole's distinctive singing is often called confectionery. Count Basie, it has even been said, should have stuck with blues-singers; also that Getz's *bossa novas* are his least interesting records. And Miles Davis is regarded by purists as a lost leader, a musician who has strayed far from jazz.

My own atitude is that each performance needs to be evaluated for what it is and on its own merits. My admiration for Louis/Satchmo's *West End Blues* and the Hot Fives and Sevens is not lessened by his material success with the infectious, toe-tapping quality of *Hello Dolly* — and *What a Wonderful World* is a well-made, agreeable record. Count Basie did not have to change the style and sound of his band to work with Sinatra. My complaint about Miles Davis, however, from the 'Bitches Brew' album onwards is not the searchings he has been involved with — and has every artistic right to undertake — but that he now plays so meagrely on his own records. Again though, if I do not particularly enjoy 'Bitches Brew', this in no way interferes with my appreciation of the towering qualities of 'Miles Ahead', 'Kind Of Blue' and 'Sketches Of Spain'.

Quincy Jones, too, started out as a working jazz player and evolved over many years with big bands before leading a band of his own. Then he continued to evolve. In more recent years he has arranged and conducted for the greatest names in popular singing; has brought about an instrumental revolution within the music industry; and moved into TV, films, publishing, artists' management and, not least, record production. This

9

subsequent career, sometimes purely musical but at others organisational or entrepreneurial, has gathered in for him more magazine and/or show-business awards than anyone else coming from this particular background. Also, it has turned him into a popular figure in his own right, a figure with 'star' status who is now as widely-known as the 'name' artists for whom he writes accompanying scores and acts as producer. At the same time those records issued solely under his own aegis always seem to enter the charts of best-sellers. It adds up to a remarkable success story.

Quincy Jones has not only aimed very high. His versatility is such that it causes one to think even in terms of 'Renaissance Man'.

Chapter 2

MORNING LIGHT

Seattle is a city of something over half a million souls situated in the northwest of the United States on an isthmus between Lake Washington and Puget Sound. It is just inside the American/Canadian border from Vancouver, while on the far horizon from the Sound are Cape Flattery and then the Pacific Ocean. Apart from Port Seattle traffic with the Orient, and being the terminal point for the Northern Pacific Railway, economically it has become best-known for its connections with the giant US aircraft industry. (Boeing build their biggest jetliners not far away at Everett.) Given its seaboard, its inland woods and lakes, and with the Rockies as a background (the invariably snow-capped Mount Baker rears to 10,778 feet) it can be a most pleasant place to live.

An unlikely place though, you might imagine, to be exporting two of the biggest names in this century's popular music, and far removed from more likely locales such as New Orleans, Chicago, New York, Detroit, Nashville, Los Angeles. But Seattle, along with Portland, Oregon, is one of the most prosperous centres of the American northwest — and as such can afford to finance its own entertainment. It is on the itineraries of all the touring artists and bands. Once upon a time they went there with the long locomotives out of Chicago. Nowadays they have the plane links. Elvis Presley's next concert prior to his fatal heart attack was due to be taking place in the main stadium there, when his backing-group and singers were ordered to turn back in the middle of their flight.

Seattle is where the story of Quincy Jones the musician really begins. . .

It was during World War II and, as Quincy recalls, 'Seattle suddenly became a place where you just ate up all kinds of music. A lot of pimps were in town, and army bases and navy bands, so it was always jumping. A lot of the Midwestern towns didn't get as much transient action as they did in Seattle — this was the war and after. It was just people moving in and

11

out all the time. I got a chance to move into all sorts of things, a gospel quartet, high school bands and stuff, marching and everything, concert bands, dance bands, Rhythm & Blues groups. Louis Armstrong came through. I got to play gigs with Billie Holiday and Cab Calloway. Oh, it was like Disneyland every day!'

In fact, he was born on 14 March, 1933 and baptised Quincy Delight Jones, Jr. That was in Chicago. But when he was eleven the family moved to Bremerton, Washington State, near Seattle, and in 1948 they moved into Seattle itself.

'This was a hell of a change for me,' he insists, in the course of a letter written to me in 1959. 'It's interesting because I went through exactly what all the fuss in the US right now is about — integration in schools. I've seen both sides. I experienced it first as a child in Chicago, where I was exposed to all kinds of gangs. 'The Vagabonds', 'The Giles A.C. Gang', 'The Dukes and Duchesses', and so on. Colour meant a lot in their constant rebellion against society, and believe me Chicago gangs were *rough*. I'll never forget when I was seven years old and saw 'Two-Gun Pete', a famous tough Chicago cop, shoot down a cat from one of the gangs and he crumpled up in front of Walgreen's Drug Store. My mind was not mature enough really to feel sympathy. I'd seen too many movies already and I just accepted it as part of Chicago life. And I accepted colour hatred as another part of it. Also I was kept busy with a part-time job, errand boy for a laundry— my first taste of responsibility!

'Summers we'd spend with my grandmother down at Louisville, Kentucky, and there I met another kind of blackness. I mean, the log-cabins and the dirt roads. We kids used to go and pull rats as big as rabbits out of the Ohio River by their tails. Grandma would skin them so we could have a gigantic fry-up. . . .

'Then, presto! A change. Out to near Seattle, I enter school—the only black kid in the class — and the other kids were wonderful to me. Positively no problems. Completely integrated. A helluva contrast to Chicago where in the gangs they dared white kids in the coloured districts and *vice versa*. It was all a lack of understanding there. Just put a white kid in a coloured school and he acts like the majority of coloured kids act. The same with a coloured/black kid in a white school. There are some traits that are more heavily instilled from childhood, but basically kids are all alike. In Seattle we used to fight together, play together, everything and it made us realise how each side was afraid of a *non-existing* element. Fear of the unknown.

'Now this isn't true everywhere in the States. In the South there is a different scene. There it's pure, unadulterated ignorance. Seattle though is a model city and the only time the colour pattern gets distorted is when an outside influence like a World War starts interfering with it. These influences can set back progress twenty years with just one scene. I feel I've experienced the integration problem. And I'm sure things would be cooler if more people had. I'll even go further and say that if people could make an effort to meet more people, inside and outside their own country, then things *would* be cooler. The enemy always looks stronger when he's far away from you. People need to get a lot closer.

'Even in Seattle, though, I used to shine shoes, do paper routes, run errands for bootleggers, pimps, prostitutes and so on. You get this everywhere. It opens your eyes to life.'

It was in Seattle too that he began to show a deeper, more genuine interest in music. 'The only music I was ever exposed to in Chicago was from the 'house rent' piano-players — long-fingered, elderly cats who just played and got juiced and ate neck-bones and red beans and rice. They all had fantastic left-hands when they played. I was very aware of this even though I was only ten.'

'As one of ten children (seven sisters, two brothers) music didn't seem too important to most of them,' Quincy adds. 'My older brother played military drums, started in jazz the same time that I did, and then quit. My father wasn't a musician, but he was the greatest inspiration I ever had. He encouraged me from the beginning, and I feel him behind me with every note I play. Or write for that matter.'

His new musical interests started with his helping to organise a small choir at the local church. His family was Catholic, but as he puts it, 'I got more of a message from the Baptist and Sanctified churches, because they used to project their feelings more. Also, I started singing spirituals under Joseph Powe, who at one time had been with Wings Over Jordan. He was at the same time leader of a US Navy dance band, and he taught me a lot about pulsation and phrasing. After singing with him I started on piano. Then I was student-manager for the Robert E. Coontz High School band and in that I experimented with clarinet, trombone, tuba, French horn, baritone, E flat alto-horn, percussion — and finally I bought a second-hand trumpet. From then on I was in every musical organisation in school until I had graduated — chorus, orchestra, dance band, etc.

'I wrote a suite called *From The Four Winds* when I was still not quite sixteen. I don't know how I knew how to do it. I'd never studied writing music. Yet I think the form, orchestration and imagination were even more mature than in some of my later works. I still can't figure it out.

Anyway, then Lionel Hampton came to Seattle, and took and started to play the suite. He wanted me to join the band and I was going to run away from home, but his wife Gladys put me off the bus and said I was too young. I just had my little be-bop bag and I was sitting there with no baggage because I couldn't go home and say I was just going to split. So Gladys pushed me off the bus and I just went back to school. Nights I'd play with Bumps Blackwell's R & B band and then be-bop after hours.

'But the suite *From The Four Winds* was quite long, more than twenty minutes, and eventually it got me a scholarship to Seattle University.'

Quincy became increasingly interested in jazz music from the age of fourteen onwards. 'It began when Cab Calloway came to play in Seattle and I was part of a local band that played opposite him. Jonah Jones was on trumpet with Cab then, and the great Milt Hinton on bass. After Cab left, Billie Holiday came and the band I was with had to accompany her. Bobby Tucker was Lady's pianist then. I've loved him ever since. He was so patient when he rehearsed us. We didn't read music too fast at that time. And afterwards Count Basie visited Seattle with his Septet. Buddy De Franco was on clarinet, Charlie Rouse on tenor-saxophone. Gus Johnson on drums. And the great Clark Terry on trumpet.'

Clark Terry later toured for nine years as the principal trumpet soloist with Duke Ellington's orchestra. Later still, when Quincy formed his own big band, he took over that solo trumpet chair for a year and, even today, he remains one of the most inventive, individual stylists on his instrument. His early influence on Quincy proved crucial. 'Clark told me how wrong I was playing and that I had a very bad lip position (I was playing under the lip). And he showed me how to get around these problems. He inspired me. His trumpet playing was so different — it had skill and soul.'

However, the biggest *overall* influence upon Quincy, other than church music and modern jazz, from those Seattle days was, without doubt, Ray Charles, the legendary singer and musician who also launched his career towards world popularity from the northwestern city. Charles (real name Ray Charles Robinson) originally hailed from Albany, Georgia — which adds poignancy to his later smash hit single *Georgia On My Mind*. Blind from the age of six, orphaned at fifteen, he worked with bands in Florida from 1948 and then made his way to Seattle in 1950. A blues singer extraordinary, he also plays piano, organ and even the alto-saxophone as well as being a gifted composer and arranger. Moreover he has the ability to impose the qualities of blues and gospel music upon other and often seemingly quite trivial themes in a way that then makes them sound soulful and authentic.

14

Also in those Seattle days Ray had a very serious problem with narcotics — something Quincy himself and his later mentor, Dizzy Gillespie, have never been into. But at the time there was no apparent effect upon his own music-making.

According to Quincy, 'Ray Charles was seventeen when I was fifteen. In Seattle he had a trio he called The Maxim Trio. It was a gas! Very modern. Played all the hip things then. And Ray used to write for a vocal group (five voices) I was with. Ernestine Anderson was our lead singer. She was very modern too and had plenty, plenty soul. One of my very first arrangements was the result of Ray telling me how to voice brass, using Billy Eckstine's *Blowin' The Blues Away* as an example. Also we would play bop together at the Elks Club. And at every jam session in Seattle there was Ray's influence as strong as a radioactive wave — it always came into them. He played alto, he could handle the clarinet, piano and he sang the end. Afterwards he went to California and recorded *Confessin' The Blues*. To me, though, his blues singing has always told the truth. My idea of a perfect marriage in jazz would be his feeling with a very full technique to project and develop it.

'Later, I was influenced by Lester Young, Dizzy Gillespie and, of course, Charlie Parker. Remember, however, this was not particularly new music to me, because in 1948 the new jazz had been in for some time and was the *only* jazz music I'd grown used to hearing on records. Consequently, I had to go back and find out what had happened before in jazz. This same situation applied to Clifford Brown, Gigi (Gryce) and many other young musicians who were not raised in the Swing era. It would account for the unbiased outlook this generation should have, being at an age where progress is yet to be seen.'

In point of fact, after graduating, Quincy received two scholarships. The first was to Seattle University, where he found the modern music department disappointing; the second was to the Schillinger House with the Berklee School of music in Boston, which 'was another gas' and where he studied for nearly a year. Sometimes he took up to ten classes a day, supplementing his grant by working as a semi-professional musician with bands in strip joints.

'Boston was the farthest I'd ever been from home, and it was close to New York.' It was there that he met Gigi Gryce for the first time. At weekends they would sneak off to New York City where he offered some of his first arrangements to bassist Oscar Pettiford, as well as having the chance 'to hit and meet Art Tatum, and Bird (Charlie Parker) and Thelonious Monk and Miles Davis, everybody. It was like a fairy story.'

15

Also there was the local school of Boston musicians including Herb Pomeroy, Charlie Mariano, and Nat Pierce. Plus, when he turned sixteen he ventured out on the road for several weeks with the Jay McShann band.

Jay 'Hootie' McShann is a hard-driving, earthy blues pianist who in the early 1980s has enjoyed another lease of popularity through his duets with the ragtime specialist Ralph Sutton ('The Last Of The Whorehouse Piano Players' LPs). Born in 1916, in the late 1930s and 1940s and usually out of Kansas City he led a series of bigger bands which for a period included Charlie Parker on alto-saxophone, the first revolutionary genius of modern jazz who cut his initial recorded solos with McShann for American Decca. Then the downfall of the corrupt political bosses in Kaycee brought Jay into a different musical involvement, closer to Rhythm & Blues.

'It was a very uncertain band with Jay not always showing up at rehearsals,' Quincy remembers. 'The drummer was Brady from California (he's been with Oscar Moore since then). The trumpeter/soloist was Eric Von Slitz from Texas and he reminded me personality-wise of Benny Bailey. The tenor player was Carruthers and he's in Los Angeles now. I don't remember the other guys. While with McShann I gained invaluable experience in writing and playing, but most of all I discovered the financial insecurity in the music business.'

Next came his remarkable stint with Lionel Hampton. 'I'd gone back to Boston when Hamp suddenly said, 'Okay, you're of age now, you can join the band'. So I left school and said I'd be back in a couple of months — I lied — thought I would at the time but I got stuck out there. The best kind of school in the world is to put the academic thing together with what's really out there. I got to meet an incredible bunch of musicians with Hampton. So I stayed nearly three years and we went to Europe in 1953 — which really opened my head up!'

Chapter 3

EUROPE

'We felt we could never leave Hamp's band because we'd got eleven guys at least who were so closely attached as friends and musicians into each other's music, we couldn't get out. Finally, at the end of 1953 everybody got scattered and went their own ways and I stayed in New York. That's when I really started in record studios. I'd recorded before that — arrangements and such — but it was really early and the Fender bass had just come out and Hampton's band was the first time they had ever used the Fender bass (Monk Montgomery, Wes' brother played it). I mention that instrument because that and the electric guitar had so much to do with what's happening now.'

QUINCY JONES

Quincy recognised early on that he was not destined to become one of the leading trumpet soloists of jazz. His great gifts and ambitions would always be connected with the overall sounds of music and the processes of composing. On the other hand, by dint of hard work and dedication he had turned himself into a trumpeter capable of playing in the brass section of any big band. This was important because now — and in the foreseeable future — such bands would provide him with the inspiration and the opportunities for his composing and arranging.

Following his stairway to 'stardom' with Benny Goodman quartets and sextets in the late 1930s, Lionel Hampton had led bands of his own which specialised in feverish excitement, even at times pandemonium. Hamp himself — whether playing vibes, two-finger piano or drums — was the epitome of high-tension showmanship and drama. His bands didn't so much swing as go on the rampage, and in the 19403, when those screaming tenor-saxophones of his were on the go, Illinois Jacquet and Arnett Cobb . . . well, anything could happen — and usually did!

However by 1953 when Hampton was forty-four, and more by accident than design, the internal personnel of the band had a strangely unorthodox character. Gladys Hampton was still doing most of the hiring and firing at this period and a lot of younger modernists had slipped into what was essentially a relic of the Swing era (albeit an indestructible one, and as always madly emotional). In the trumpet section, apart from veteran lead Walter Williams, Quincy — nearly two years out of music college and still on a peppercorn salary — found himself sitting beside Benny Bailey and the rapidly developing Art Farmer. Then, a few months before the European tour of 1953 Clifford Brown joined (replacing Bailey). Clifford was already a solo voice to be reckoned with, and his approach to playing jazz fitted in entirely with Quincy's attitude in writing it. Quincy decided that he was the one man on trumpet he really wanted to write for, and he continued to do so until the time of Brownie's death in the car-crash of 1956.

In a letter to me just before that tragic event Quincy wrote, 'About Clifford Brown, I'll put it like this. If any musician of the present day can be compared with Parker, it's Clifford. I can honestly say that his is the most unblossomed talent of this generation. He should not only be judged by his present talent (which is still of superior quality) but by its potentialities. Charlie Parker and Dizzy and all the other influences were not judged until they reached maturity. It takes a young musician many years to rid the mind of *clichés* and to unscramble the millions of young ideas into what it takes to make a mature and original musical influence. By knowing Clifford very well, I'm aware of his sensitivity and superior taste; he will *never* lower his standards and play without sincerely feeling, whatever the mood. He is a young musician in age but already a comparatively mature one in ideas. When he matures in his own standards I do believe he will be a major jazz influence. He is the kind of person who would excel at anything attempted. (He plays as much piano now as he does trumpet.) You can rest assured that all the Dizzy and Navarro influences will not be present in the mature Brownie. Remember, Dizzy began by imitating Roy Eldridge.'

When I first met Quincy in London in 1956 I suggested he could write a good *memoir* of his time with the band, including a section about its most extraordinary leader. But he shook his head. 'I'm sorry. It would take three or four chapters of a book even to start on all the weird things Hamp used to do. And I couldn't give you the reasons for them. I mean the guy's a jazz natural, and at the same time is a very unpredictable man and musician. I loved him. But he's definitely more than a character. . .' When they played at the Bandbox in NYC (next door to Birdland), Hamp dressed them in Bermuda shorts, purple jackets and Tyrolian hats. And when they played *Flying Home* he marched them out to play in the street!

18

'I was so hip then it was pitiful,' Quincy recalls, 'and Brownie and I would stop to tie our shoes or somehing, because outside Birdland in the intermission there'd be Monk and Dizzy and Bud Powell, all the be-bop idols saying *What is this shit? You'd do anything for a gimmick!'*

Nevertheless, with Hampton's band Quincy had moved into the very forefront of big bands (incidentally, *Kingfish,* the first composition of his which Hamp recorded, contains a rare instance of Quincy playing a trumpet solo) and he discovered that he needed to start looking after his music. Today, he has his own large and active publishing house and his compositions are fully protected.

On 2 September, 1953 the band left New York for Oslo and the beginning of a lengthy European tour. Only a week before Clifford Brown had recorded an LP for Blue Note under his own name; included on it were Quincy's *Wailbait* and a new ballad the latter had just written called *Brownie Eyes.* However, it was after the Hampton men reached Europe that the composer/arranger kept the recording companies as busy as a disturbed ants' nest. He was playing a concert each evening, sometimes a matinee as well — and often travelling a considerable distance between venues. Even so, Gigi Gryce and Quincy wrote prolifically, both in Paris and in Stockholm and all places in between. As Alun Morgan summed it up in *Jazz Monthly,* 'the Hampton bandsmen made more recordings in Europe than any previous touring group. Furthermore the recordings revealed a literally astonishing amount of jazz talent and helped to set a number of hitherto unrecognised musicians in correct perspective.'

When I visited Paris in June 1954 with Alun Morgan, the French Vogue Records' office had still not recovered from the impact of Quincy. Al Ferrari of Vogue, a former saxophone-player, gave it to me quite straight-forwardly: 'Last year we had a remarkable young man here, by the name of Quincy Jones. He wrote all the time.' Apparently, after each concert with Hampton ended, he regularly stayed up all night writing. And nothing, but nothing, perturbed him. If he arrived in the recording studios to find more musicians there than his score had anticipated he simply sat down and wrote out the additional parts on the spot. He could write anytime anywhere. He went with Gigi Gryce to one of the Swedish sessions, and their scores were still unfinished. The studio contained only one piano. Gigi immediately sat down at it to finish his scores. Quincy sat down in the far corner and despite the crash of experimental piano chords going on about his ears, and the talking and tuning up by the other musicians as they arrived, he finished his work on a few scraps of manuscript.

'And he writes the kind of arrangements that musicians like to play,'

Borje Ekberg, the chief of Swedish Metronome, told Alun Morgan. 'Most of our sessions with the Hampton boys had to be held very late at night or early in the morning after the public concerts and naturally the musicians were tired. But when they saw Quincy's scores they all said, Hell! This is great. Come on, let's make it!'

In Paris, Quincy composed for octets, septets and sextets, and for a seventeen-piece band with Americans and Frenchmen mixed. In Stockholm, he composed for the brass soloists of the Hampton band, Clifford Brown especially, and for a band built around pianist George Wallington. But all of these sessions took place in an atmosphere of intrigue, for Hamp (urged on by Gladys and other outside influences) had stipulated that no member of the band could record independently in Europe. Anyone caught doing so, it was added by Mrs Hampton, would be fired, instantly, and with no return passage money back to the States. It was necessary, therefore, that the musicians make their way to the pre-arranged sessions without the powers-that-were knowing. . .

At the outset this was easy enough. When the band arrived in Stockholm from Oslo the first session was set for the morning of 14 September. The several Hampton men called left their hotel singly and at irregular intervals, later to reassemble in the Metronome Studios. At this session Quincy played piano within the background parts to an Annie Ross vocalised verson of *Jackie*, originally a tenor-saxophone solo by Wardell Gray; and also on Gigi Gryce's score of Jerome Kern's ballad, *The Song Is You* for Miss Ross. Then he worked on two longer scores of his own featuring George Wallington with a Swedish band. *'Round About Midnight*, Thelonious Monk's best-known theme was first — and in Quince's darkly brooding orchestration one has a model of mood evocation as portrayed by a small group. A Wallington original, *Blue Bird*, came after it, and into this Quincy introduced a more conventional swing pattern. Outstanding in the band with Wallington was trombonist Ake Persson.

It was then time for the Hampton men to leave for a rehearsal of the band's evening concert. Quincy promised, though, that he would be back at midnight with three scores to feature Clifford Brown and Art Farmer in front of the Swedish band.

This time it was less easy. Hamp by now suspected that some form of recording was going on. He was not staying with the other musicians but fuelled by Gladys, when the men went back to their hotel after the concert they found George Hart, the band's road manager, posted in a large armchair in the foyer with orders to stop any musicians leaving the premises that night with their instruments. Quincy and Clifford and Art complained of tiredness and went to their rooms. There they sat in complete frustration until nearly midnight; and still the road manager as reported by other bandsmen, hadn't moved. The let-out came when one of them thought of the fire-escape running by a window at the end of the corridor. Delighted, the three felt their way down it in the darkness and were off to the session.

It was at this session that Quincy introduced his melodic and intriguing *Stockholm Sweetnin'*, his first jazz classic. Both trumpeters made outstanding use of it, Farmer playing in the near-Miles Davis style which he has since left behind, and Brownie already himself. Quincy later commented: 'I consider this one of Brownie's most well-constructed solos on record, and in itself serves as a stimulating, inspired composition'. Also, he penned *'Scuse These Bloos*, revealing his clear understanding of the old and the new in jazz, plus a score of the standard *Falling In Love With Love*. The session ended with the trumpeters jamming on *Lover Come Back To Me*.

After Stockholm the band went to Brussels and then on to Paris. It was here that Annie Ross was told by Gladys Hampton that she had to leave the band. Stories converge to the effect that the agents for the tour and one influential critic, the late Hugues Panassié, had been telling the leader and his wife that a white singer with a black band wouldn't please French audiences. Panassié was a most bigoted man, as printed examples of his views indicate — 'Charlie Parker . . . an extremely gifted musician, who gradually gave up jazz in favour of be-bop'; 'Dizzy Gillespie . . . began to experiment with a style of his own and abandoned the traditional music of his race in favour of an instrumental technique and harmonic intervals drawn from the study of European music'; and 'J.J. Johnson, an excellent trombonist and a soloist full of imagination, but who has recently degenerated under the influence of bop musicians'. Anyway, his further opinion that white jazz performers were by nature inferior most regrettably prevailed, and so Annie went. Whereupon, out of anger and in sympathy George Wallington walked off the stand with her. (He then agreed to make a solo LP for French Vogue which gave him his air fare back to New York). At subsequent dates Quincy shared the piano chores with Hamp — and it was clear that the latter greatly regretted having been swayed into going along with the decision. As he told Quincy: 'From now on I begin to run my own band and ignore these damn' agents. . .'

The recordings also began again, and with them the moonlighting. George Hart was still shadowing suspected musicians, in particular Clifford Brown. The musicians in turn, who wanted to showcase their playing and at the same time augment their salaries, enlisted the aid of French Vogue's recording staff, in whom the cunning of a wartime underground movement and a natural Armenian business acumen still flourished. These men (and women), by an elaborate system of decoys, ensured that the musicians made the sessions.

At the first of these, on 26 September, two Jones scores were recorded. *Purple Shades* featured Anthony Ortega, the Hampton lead-alto. *La Rose Noire*, based on the harmonies of George Gershwin's *Summertime*, featured trumpet, trombone, alto, tenor, baritone, flute, rhythm, and its young composer on piano. It is a good example of the way Quincy can write a delicate and beautiful score and still cause it to swing.

Ironically, two day's later Lionel Hampton himself was invited by the Hot Club de France to a party at the Ecole Normale de la Musique Supérieure. The saturnine Panassié was attending also. It turned into a unique occasion at which the champagne never ceased to flow. And before a selected audience of friends and musicians Lionel devised a jam session which included such different musicians as Mezz Mezzrow, Alix Combelle and his own band's guitarist Billy Mackell. As the party progressed so Lionel himself improvised brilliantly on the vibraphone. (*Blue Panassié* is one of the greatest of his preserved solos.) Previously, French Vogue had asked if they might tape the proceedings and been told to 'go right ahead'. These were shrewd and aggressive tactics on their part. For apart from gaining a Hampton LP, it meant that the coast would be clear for Gigi Gryce and Quincy to organise their big band session (including ten Hampton men) in a studio the other side of Paris.

But then this other, parallel session nearly never took place. Hamp, quite innocently, invited lead-trumpet Walter Williams and the brilliant young trombonist Jimmy Cleveland along to the Hot Club party, two men who were vital to the Gryce/Jones big band. To refuse the invitation would have aroused added suspicion, so they told Gigi to rehearse his band and wait for them. They went to the party, jammed a bit with Lionel, and waited for the champagne to take over. Then, in the mounting excitement, they slid away, jumped into a taxi and raced over to join the big band.

Quincy's *Keepin' Up With Jonesy*, recorded that day, is perhaps the outstanding performance by a Franco-American band in existence. (Its only rival, the Gryce score of *Brown Skins*, features Clifford in both slow and faster veins.) The composition has a double theme. The first, of 32 bars, is stated by pianist Henri Renaud and the rhythm section. The second, a supple variation on the first, is then taken up by the whole band. A muted trumpet chase follows beten Brownie and Art Farmer, and solos by Gryce, Cleveland and tenorman Clifford Solomon before Quincy draws out a marvellous climax in brass. The whole piece, lasting some seven minutes, is characterised by a very Basie-like beat.

Hamp took the band on tour through France after this and it wasn't until 9 October that the other, undercover big band reassembled to record Quincy's *Bum's Rush* and a further Gryce score. On the following day Gigi with a small group recorded Quincy's lovely *Evening In Paris*.

The last of these scattered sessions occurred on 10 November, after the band had returned to Stockholm. Quincy asked four Hampton men to these sessions: Clifford Brown, Art Farmer, Jimmy Cleveland and drummer Alan Dawson. These, together with five Swedish musicians again including Ake Persson. Then Clifford Brown received a telegram from the American Federation of Musicians expressly forbidding him to record in Sweden without Lionel Hampton's permission. Quince had written a feature-piece for him called *Pogo Stick* (Pogo being Brownie's nickname with the other players) but decided it was wiser to let him stand down. As he says, 'You can't go against the Union. They fight for you, so you have to respect and obey them'. The others made the session, Art Farmer pretending to the road manager he was ill and confined to his room. They recorded *Pogo Stick, Jones Bones, Liza* and jammed *Sometimes I'm Happy*, Farmer in particular contributing a series of wonderfully-conceived solos — for a sick man!

The tour ended and the rest of the band flew back to the States in advance of Hampton. Eleven of its members, knowing they faced the sack when the records came to be issued, promptly resigned, leaving Gladys Hampton in a rage and Hamp himself, for the first time in his career as a leader, almost without a band. 'I wanted to settle down in New York and arrange,' Quincy explains. 'My little girl was born at this time. I was so broke, mind you, that if a trip around the world had cost a nickel, *I* couldn't have paid the fare to get across the street!'

But he did settle down to arrange. In the next couple of years the only trumpet he played was in the section of a pair of recording sessions with Dizzy Gillespie and on a CBS-TV series with Ray Anthony through the summer of 1954. He began to arrange for everyone who mattered though, or so it seemed. Another letter he sent me in 1955 read: 'New York has about as much work as an arranger could ask for, believe it or not. I'm freelancing a lot, doing jazz and commercial recordings. Fortunately, the Artist & Repertoire man, Marv Holtzman, that I work for at Columbia (CBS) is a very jazz-conscious guy, and is more than considerate in letting me have as much freedom in jazz as possible, so I have to co-operate with a smile when he does a commercial date. He's letting me do a big band record under my own name, the first.

'And yet . . . in a year's time maybe nobody will be working. I guess by now you've heard about Bird.' Charlie 'Yardbird' Parker had died a month before. 'What are all the cats going to play since he can't make any more records? There was a big benefit for his kids at Carnegie Hall last week. It raised $13,000. It's too bad they didn't give that kind of money to him when he was alive. Financial insecurity was one of the chief causes of his death.'

Quincy arranged a series of albums for musicians he much admired — Clark Terry, his first decisive trumpet teacher, altoist Sonny Stitt (a magnificent solo collection on Roost Records), George Wallington, Oscar Pettiford and later, Julian 'Cannonball' Adderley. He even did some arranging for Lionel Hampton, the rumpus over the European tour having finally died down. But then he had a major disappointment. The big band album of his own he had been promised by Columbia failed to materialise. He made the first session, with nineteen men, and then the interested artist and repertoire man either left or was forced out of the company. No one offered to carry on with the project. To my knowledge the main tapes of that first session are still gathering dust in the CBS vaults. So he got on with writing dates for La Vern Baker, Chuck Willis, The Clovers.

And then one day he walked home from another, commercial recording session and his wife said: 'Dizzy Gillespie's been on the 'phone. He kept talking about the desert. . .'
So what kind of a musician had Quincy become by and at this point?

An instinctive one, certainly, and one who very much believed in groove, in feeling, in sincere excitement; who was influenced by black church music, by Ray Charles, Basie and Ellington, the be-bop of Parker and Gillespie and not least the almost vocalised sounds of the best jazz improvisation. 'I'm sure,' he wrote to me then, 'that jazz will not be furthered by long analytical speeches of accomplishment. It will always be sparked by emotion, warmth, heart and a certain intellectual content that is not overdone. Without emotional and rhythmic feeling, jazz is not jazz. Borrowing classical techniques to further this feeling of progressing jazz, but trying to put it on the same level as these techniques is retarding it. There has been a tendency in America of late to stress classical airs in many of the jazz works. In doing this, a lot of musicians have missed the message altogether. In short, when we stop swinging, we're competing with Ravel, Bartók, Stravinsky and a number of other brilliant musicians on their own ground . . . musicians who easily outdo us there. Jazz must develop its

24

own language.'

This was, and still remains, a determining factor in his music-making.

Again, although at one time or another Quincy has played all the chief brass instruments, and in particular with several of the greatest trumpet teams in the world, he does not look back on these experiences in terms of purely personal playing. Instead he looks back to the extra insight they gave him into the ways of brass players — how they think, how they feel, how they are best utilised in written passages.

As a result he writes exceedingly well for brass. Wendell Culley, for so long a trumpeter with Count Basie and before that with Lionel Hampton, singled out Quincy for this from all other orchestrators he had ever known. As he put it to me, 'Quincy . . . has so vivid an imagination that he can scare you with his brass writing at times. And yet, when you get down to playing it, you find he's written things which appeal to the trumpeter. It's because he knows the instrument himself and fully understands the physical problems of it. Some writers, who only know the theory side of the trumpet, will demand that you play vicious shock notes the whole time and that can soon wear you lip out. Quincy doesn't do it that way. He actually notates a passage as the trumpet would naturally feel it.'

Always, then, Quincy's understanding of instruments is the servant of his composing and arranging. 'The orchestra is the most fascinating instrument I've played,' he says. 'It has more dimensions than a solo instrument.' On the other hand, he has approached the orchestra with something of the head-and-heart playing of the great users of solo instruments in jazz, of Louis Armstrong, Parker, Dizzy Gillespie. And he had the experience of once sitting beside Clifford Brown and Art Farmer.

'I like to look on the orchestra as *my* personal instrument, the same as the soloist looks on his, and I like to improvise with it,' he explains. 'I like it to describe my feelings, my moods and my thoughts, so that writing becomes the same as improvising for me. Naturally, I have to consider form too, even more than the soloist does; also, I have to consider the individual personalities of the guys I'm writing for, but I still like to have the feeling of an improvisation in the writing. Form alone is not enough in jazz writing. [Duke] Ellington has always impressed me with the improvised feeling he writes into his work. The only way to write this feeling into a score is to let the head and the heart work together. If the head works alone then the score usually sounds contrived, even with the best craftsmanship. If the heart works with the head, though, the score becomes more of a living thing. All your feelings are able to flow freely. All your thoughts too. In effect, you tell the truth about yourself, and the truth doesn't need to

25

hurt. Jazz has always been a man telling the truth about himself.'

In Quincy's up-tempo writing, where intelligence and passion mingle and further each other, there is always a thoroughly emotional verve — a verve which erupts as soon as the musicians play over their parts and which recalls the spontaneous combustion of a big band 'head' arrangement at its best (after all, what is a 'head' arrangement if it isn't a suddenly desired and conceived ensemble improvisation?). It is, of course, the pragmatic attitude as well of his scores which most clearly expresses this verve — an attacking attitude in the ensemble passages, which are made to speak in a very direct way, and in the underlying pulsation, which is left freely flowing. 'He writes with such a natural swing,' the Swedish altoist Arne Domnerus has said, 'that it seems like his compositions more or less play themselves.'

Of the head's contribution Quincy is more than conscious. This is because he has to select from his thoughts, and then shape and stabilise them on paper. 'There are the parts of writing that are only arrived at as a result of knowledge,' he says. 'The construction and continuity of a work. Then the orchestrating of it. In orchestrating a work, if I use a voicing that hasn't been heard from me before, or a texture, it's a result of musical knowledge. And composition itself is a result of musical knowledge used with imagination.' At the same time, he notates the ensemble passages with instinctive timing and rhythmic feeling and these he claims to know only through their existence and effect. 'I prefer not to ask too many questions when it's an affair of the heart,' he replies disarmingly. 'It's there and I'm grateful it's there. I prefer not to ask why or when it came to be there.'

His knowledge of the orchestra, and of its possible sub-divisions, is full and far-reaching and allows him to write with an easy exactness. Also, he can write a brilliantly detailed score that appears to the casual listener to have a simple spontaneity. An illustration of this is the lightly but firmly ensembled passages that accompany Dizzy Gillespie's *I Can't Get Started* solo; another is the small, trumpet-led ensemble, set against the larger ensemble which introduces the theme of *Jessica's Day;* or the few fearless outbursts of brass at the close of *Night In Tunisia* — all parts of Dizzy Gillespie's 'World Statesman' LP on Verve.

But while he is a fluent, and fast, orchestrator (arranger), Quincy regards this proficiency as essentially an aid to the demands of a composition. Unlike Duke Ellington, he does not consider the orchestral scoring necessarily an integral part of the composition, although the composition itself is vital to any orchestration. He prefers to compose, or to take

26

another's composition, and then to orchestrate, to have the melody and its harmonisation settled before thinking about portraying them through the orchestra. Orchestration for its own sake does not interest him. He orchestrates only to enhance the composition. He uses instrumentation and sounds if and when they are right for the compositon, never just for effect. In view of which it is not surprising to discover that as a composer he is naturally a melodist. He has not greatly concerned himself with advancing form in music; in fact, when composing blues and ballads or, for that matter, music either bullish or beautiful, he appears content to work within their traditional forms. But he tackles the making up of a new melody line with two clearly defined aims.

The first is that it must have an intrinsic strength and substance — allowing it to exist as the better popular songs do, facing a series of widely varied interpretations without losing its own identifiable character. The second is that it must have suppleness and, at the same time, harmonic completeness; for without these combined qualities it cannot act out its life force, or inspire an orchestra and its soloists.

To realise these aims Quincy selects from a rich imagination. It is a careful selection though, applying order and logic to the basic profusion of the imagination. Even when finding the arrangement easy and fast, he is a deliberately slower composer. Usually the ideas for a melody come to him suddenly, at the precise moment when he least expects them. He enjoys this: 'A relaxed and not a forced imagination. Ideas are unusual in that they *never* come when you sit down and try hard to have them,' he explains. 'They come when you're walking down the street, or maybe just drinking a cup of coffee . . . then you have to reach for a newspaper or a menu card to note them down.' However, with the selection from these ideas, and the shaping of them, he elects to take his time. Often he will spend six months thinking about a melody before he is satisfied with it. 'I have to think about the making of a composition from my ideas, shaping the melodic line and the chord changes that go with it,' he says. 'Although the ideas for the melody may be strong, I still have to portray them at their best, and I shape them in many different ways before I finalise them in one.' By the end of this period of incubation, though, a melody of significance usually emerges. *Evening In Paris* and at least a dozen other themes from his earlier years are already classics of their kind. Even so, his method is different from that of, say, Django Reinhardt, who would escape for a day's fishing and come back with a *Nuages* or *Manoir Des Mes Rêves* complete in his head.

Another reason, perhaps, for Quincy's taking his time is the actual length of his melodic lines. Many jazz and other composers are satisfied with short, staccato-type figures which they repeat several times with only slight alterations to make the main 8-bar or 16-bar phrases. Quincy's melodic phrases are longer and often require the entire 8 or 16 bars to unfold, for they have a more river-like run about them. One of his ballads, *The Midnight Sun Never Sets* (written in 1958, and first recorded with a sixteen-piece Swedish orchestra) demonstrates this: its lines, so finely apportioned take shape slowly in an entirely legato way.

When he uses the 32-bar song structure, he achieves a flowing quality throughout the composition, for the line of the middle 8-bar phrase (or release) is always closely connected with that of the main 8 bars and skilfully linked with it, thereby attributing a strong continuity to the overall chorus. *Stockholm Sweetnin'* (written in 1953, and first recorded with Clifford Brown in Sweden) is this *exactly;* it has a smooth and uninterrupted melodic development, the key-change into the middle 8 bars notwithstanding, and from the muted opening to its splendidly-effected climax in the last 4 bars is a continuous tribute to the composer's willpower and reasoning.

A further point about Quincy the melodist concerns his lyricism. For, while his strong sense of melodic continuity confirms this, it in no way exaggerates it. And his lyricism, as a songlike quality, is a deep and powerful force within him. It affects all his work (even the more animated blues, where as an artifice it could never be applied). It contributes enormously to the long and alternately exciting or exquisite lines he writes, mellowing and enriching their contours, and adding a sense of almost joyous well-being to their expression. And yet, at the same time it is a firm lyricism, untouched by the overt sentimentality which ruins the work of so many 'pop' songwriters. Such lyricism is rare in jazz too. Miles Davis in his most exalted moments has it and Milt Jackson nearly always; but fewer among the composers, other than Ellington and Gil Evans and Gerry Mulligan. So that Quincy's already melodically distinctive work is rendered even more so because of it.

It is difficult to communicate the huge suggestiveness of a musical spirit like Quincy Jones's. As John Cowper Powys has said about analysing an artist, in this case Rabelais, 'There are certain great men who make their critics feel even as children, who picking up stray wreckage and broken shells from the edge of the sea waves, return home to show their companions *what the sea is like*'. However: I have tried in this book to collect a little 'from the edge of the sea waves' towards such an end.

One aspect of his composing/arranging, which I must also collect here briefly, is his belief that jazz music need not go outside its own resources in order to develop interestingly. Some musicians disagree with him. They believe jazz needs to integrate with European music. For in jazz, as in life, there are those who develop the existing order and there are those who despair of developing it. The natural resources of jazz, and where they can be taken to, Quincy believes, are so vast and so deep that there is no likelihood of their being exhausted.

'A natural growth, and from the natural resources,' he says. 'It's the only way to progress jazz. It's the only way anyone ever has progressed jazz. It can't exist on other people's resources. And why should it need to, after its own have given it nearly a century of creative development with the prospect of many more years to come? I'm still for a natural growth. I'll use all I know in music to assist, but at the same time it has to use its own resources.'

Chapter 4

DIZZY FOR THE WORLD

Following an initial exchange of letters, I first came face-to-face with Quincy Jones in 1957, underneath the clock at, of all places, Waterloo Station in London.

I defined him then in my mind as a compact, finely-featured young man, almost an eagle, with bright eyes, a determined mouth, and quick, animated gestures. His talk about music, once started, was a fast flow, touching on many shores, and all the time carrying with it the remarkable flotsam and jetsom of his experiences. Also — and significantly — he was accompanied on this occasion by Bobby Tucker, once the pianist for Billie Holiday, but by this time working with Billy Eckstine.

Later, at a restaurant just along the street from the present Ronnie Scott's, Quince talked with obviously deep affection for his young daughter. 'She's a beautiful monster,' he told us. 'Only last week we were fast asleep and she came into the bedroom and switched on our TV. It still didn't wake us. So she got a big packet of crackers and slowly but surely ground them into the bed. Man, you can't sleep on broken biscuits. . .' However on this same subject Bobby (Tucker) wasn't going to be upstaged: 'So I am sleeping in after a long, late gig with Billy,' he said. 'And *my* daughter wanted to get *me* up. She'd tried pulling my eyelids back — still without making me move. So then she suddenly appeared at the edge of the bed with a dripping wet towel, just about to dump it on my face. I knew she wasn't tall enough to reach the washbasin. It could have come from only one other place. I was out of bed in a *flash!*'

The two men were later to work together in close harmony when Quincy began to arrange for Billy Eckstine. Tucker, as Mister B's established musical director, became the younger man's invaluable adviser. 'It's funny,' he said to me, 'I've only ever had two regular jobs in my professional working life and they've both been called Bill.'

At our next meeting I examined Quincy's leather travelling grip. As if in defiance of the grey July day, it was bright with colour, stuck over with labels of all sizes and shapes from the different countries where music had taken him. At first I thought the grip must have served several musicians, but they all tied in with Quincy's movements, and little by little, pausing over first one and then another, I followed through the pattern of his (till then) working life. First, the American cities he had passed through with Lionel Hampton as a musical apprentice from the age of seventeen; then Canada and Mexico, Paris and Western Europe, the Scandinavian countries, and North Africa — the extent of his 1953 touring with Hampton. Athens, the Middle East and on to Pakistan with Dizzy Gillespie's band; then back to New York before setting off on a South American tour with Gillespie. Each told of something achieved, of a new contact. The last batch of labels proclaimed his return to Paris, as staff arranger for Barclay Records and with the intention of studying in private with the legendary Nadia Boulanger, musical and spiritual leader for a number of the world's finest composers — and who, in her turn would introduce the young American to her French contemporary Olivier Messiaen.

And he was still only twenty-five years of age!

Pointing at the grip again, I remarked — slightly obviously — on the many labels he had collected in just a few short months with Dizzy's big band. He said 'yes' to this, and then, almost without realising it, I was led into a whole load of questions about this band. Not awkward questions as it transpired, because Quincy has a retentive memory — and he is easy in conversation, with an alert way of speaking and a quick sense of humour; but questions nevertheless that led 'backstage' where this unique band was concerned — to find out, albeit posthumously, about the role he had played as its musical director.

To preface these questions though, and Q's many intriguing answers, let me mention a few background facts. In the first place, the 1956 tour of the Middle East by the Dizzy Gillespie band was sponsored by the United States Government. The State Department, recognising at last that jazz music was an important cultural export, and a means of improving international relations, authorised The American National Theatre Academy to send a sizeable jazz unit overseas as part of its $2,500,000 propaganda programme. It was Professor Marshall Stearns, founder of The Institute of Jazz Studies in New York, who suggested building a big band around Dizzy Gillespie, the greatest modern trumpeter, and at the time without a band of his own. This was ultimately approved, and Stearns himself was retained as a lecturer to go with the band. Plans went ahead for the party to leave New York in the late spring of 1956.

Because the State Department had agreed to underwrite the difference between the tour's costs and its subsidised receipts, the band had a sure start. It missed meeting up with those characters, straight out of the pages of Damon Runyon, who so often get their untrustworthy clutches on a big band venture. The money was there to pay for arrangements, uniforms, travel tickets, everything. Salaries for sidemen were to be generous, and this too was important, for it meant that the band would have noteworthy soloists which other big bands (Ellington and Basie apart) could hardly have afforded.

But there was one problem: the non-availability of Gillespie himself at the time the band was to go into rehearsal.

Though overjoyed at the prospect of fronting another big band (and at a salary rumoured to equal that of the then US President Eisenhower) the trumpeter was contracted to tour Europe in the spring of 1956 with Norman Granz's 'Jazz At The Philharmonic' group. After much debate it was agreed finally that Dizzy should make the tour with Granz — and that in his absence the actual organisation of the new band be given over to a deputy, Quincy Jones. The latter, while already arranging for the band, and busily practising trumpet after hardly touching the instrument in two years, had to find time not only to hire the musicians but then go down and rehearse them.

RH: Those must have been the busiest few weeks of your life, even more so than when you were in Europe with Hampton.

QJ: So right. I was kept as busy as a one-armed paperhanger with lice. I scored *Jessica's Day, Rockin' Chair, The Champ, School Days, I Can't Get Started, Night In Tunisia* and *Hey, Pete* (which we used to play with the stage-lights off during the Middle East tour).

RH: Ernie Wilkins also scored for the band — *Dizzy's Business*, adapted from a movement of 'The Drum Suite', was one of his I seem to remember. And *Doodlin'*, the Horace Silver blues. Was he able to take charge of any of the rehearsals for you?

QJ: No. Ernie was busy making 'The Drum Suite' and the Andy Kirk albums for RCA Victor. I was even lucky to get him to rehearsals. And up until a week before leaving, deep inside I was not sure about Ernie making the tour — but he didn't let me down. I had the rehearsal headache alone for two weeks, planning two concert programmes, getting the music written and getting it right with the band. Lorraine, Dizzy's wife, was of great assistance though. And she was behind me all the way, in every decision I made.

32

RH: Whereabouts in New York did the band do its rehearsing?

QJ: At Ames's Studios on 52nd and 7th Avenue.

RH: Were the musicians paid by the State Department at this stage, or did they have to fit the rehearsals between other paid work?

QJ: The rehearsals were paid for, fortunately — and this helped to get the full respect of all the musicians involved. But the payments were almost cut the last week — a misunderstanding on some official's part. Four days to go before the tour started and the money stopped! We made it though.

RH: Then there was the problem of several musicians you wanted for the band not being available at the time of the tour.

QJ: Well, the original band Dizzy and I decided on in New York had Idrees Sulieman and Ermet Perry with Carl Warwick as the other trumpets; Melba Liston, Jimmy Cleveland and Frank Rosolino, trombones; Gigi Gryce, Ernie Wilkins, Lucky Thompson, Jerome Richardson and Sahib Shihab, saxophones; Walter Bishop, piano; Nelson Boyd, bass; Charlie Persip, drums; and a Cuban conga drummer called 'Potato'.

Anyway, it was a good idea — too damn' good. Money, previous commitments, and a thousand and one other reasons prevented me moulding it into a band with these men. All kinds of guys were hitting on to me to get places in the band, of course, and half of them were probably great but I had to be sure — there was no room for any chances. Lucky Thompson couldn't get back from Paris in time. Gigi Gryce changed his mind about going after he'd already called one replacement, who'd called another replacement. Finally, in desperation, I called Phil Woods long-distance on the Birdland tour, and he accepted the alto solo book.

When the band was finally settled I had Ermet Perry, Joe Gordon, Carl Warwick and myself as the trumpets; Melba Liston, Frank Rehak and Rod Levitt, trombones; Phil Woods, Jimmy Powell, Ernie Wilkins, Billy Mitchell and Marty Flax, saxophones and the same rhythm section as planned.

I happened on several of the men quite accidentally. Rod Levitt had played in my band in Seattle. I hadn't seen him in five or six years, and then one day I was walking home and met him in the street in New York. There and then I asked him if he'd go on the Middle East tour with Dizzy Gillespie. At first he thought I was crazy. But I knew he was a good bass-trombonist and a wonderful musician too. So I asked him again. When he realised I was serious he agreed.

For tenor I first tried to get Budd Johnson. Then he became contractor for Benny Goodman's band, so that was that. I tried to find Benny Golson, on tour in Florida with Earl Bostic — no luck. Jerome Richardson had accepted, but between times he was called by The Roxy house band, one of the first Negroes ever to be in the band there. I couldn't halt that kind of progress, could I? Finally, I thought of a guy I'd heard on records and at sessions at The Bluebird in Detroit. It was a long shot, but worth a try. Billy Mitchell he was called. I sat down at the phone to call Thad Jones who'd played with him in Detroit and who I thought might have his number. Suddenly the phone rang on me, and who should it be but Billy! Cannonball Adderley had passed through Detroit with his band and told Billy about my problem. So he was hired. Joe Gordon was with Herb Pomeroy's big band in Boston, and I stole him! Dizzy had set Melba Liston and the rhythm section before he left for Europe. And Carl Warwick was an old childhood buddy of his.

RH: Did you have to turn away anyone you'd have liked to have in the band?

QJ: Yeah — but after it was too late. Then as you'd expect, I had offers from all kinds of guys! Milt Hinton was one. Wow!

RH: That must have been a real disappointment. But with the kind of shouting brass figures that Wilkins and A.K. Salim and Melba Liston as well as you yourself were writing for the band, how exactly did you distribute the demanding lead-trumpet parts?

QJ: Ermet Perry played most of the lead parts. He's built like a rock. Joe Gordon played lead on *Cool Breeze*. I played lead on *I Can't Get Started*, behind Dizzy's solo, *My Reverie, Flamingo* and *Yesterdays* — all the ballads, in fact, because my chops were tired. Rehak played all the trombone leads (great too!)

RH: I noticed that Dizzy had all the trumpet section change to the 45-degree angle instrument he'd developed. With all its bells pointing upwards and outwards like that, the section must have disseminated its sounds better.

QJ: I found the 45-degree angle horn better for reading with too. And it added a third to the top register. I got pretty used to it after a while.

RH: After the right musicians — the men you knew would make it musically — you had to find out at the rehearsals if they got on together as people. What I mean is, a collection of great performers doesn't of necessity make a great team — if they can't get on together as human beings. And yet you can't apply too much discipline, simply because they are human beings.

QJ: There were no real flare-ups. The guys were on guard, and turned out to be the best-disciplined band I ever fronted at rehearsals. I even remember most of the guys showing up for rehearsals at the height of the blizzards with arms full of injections. (No, not dope! We had no narcotics problems with the band, but shots for typhoid, etc.) We got an almost impossible job done, thanks to their enthusiasm.

RH: What route did you take when the band left New York?

QJ: We left New York, by air and picked up Dizzy in Rome. He was there waiting at the airport with his 45-degree angle horn out — and playing *Sweet Lorraine* for his wife, who'd come with us. He had no idea who was in the band until we got out of the 'plane. It was funny when he saw cats like Joe Gordon and Billy Mitchell — he was quite surprised. Once the tour began Dizzy solidified the band's morale. It was as if a flock of sheep had found its shepherd at last. And Dizzy's sense of humour knows no limits.

RH: And then it was on to work in the more intense heat of the Middle East?

QJ: Yes. So right. We balled all the way down to Abadan, Persia — Dacca, Pakistan — Karachi, Pakistan — Beirut, Lebanon — Damascus, Syria — one other city in or near Syria, I forget the name of it — Ankara, Turkey — Instanbul, Turkey — Belgrade, Yugoslavia — Zagreb, Yugoslavia — and finally, Athens. Flying all the way of course.

RH: Was there any one in particular to look after the band while it was there? You know, the baggage and that sort of thing. A band's just like a cricket team really.

QJ: Yes. Dizzy's cousin, Boo Frazier (*Boo's Blues*). He was a disc-jockey in North Carolina and he took a leave of absence to be our bandboy. He's a groovy little cat too. There wasn't a lot of work for him to do though. We all hung out together a lot.

RH: The audience-reception must have varied quite perceptibly between the cities visited. Often you were representing the culture of the newest civilisation in the world in cities with cultural traditions of their own going back many thousands of years. And political attitudes too. When you played in Athens the anti-Western feeling over Cyprus was at its worst.

QJ: Athens was the most *un*musical of the cities we went to. But in the end even the Greek audiences got with us. On the other hand, Belgrade was a bitch. There was a wonderful radio orchestra there which we loved to listen to. The musicians were very warm and friendly. They reminded us very much of musicians in New York, which was surprising, because the Yugoslavs have only been allowed to dig jazz for the past few years.

RH: Which reminds me of Marshall Stearns's story of the communist party member in Yugoslavia who, after meeting the band, exclaimed in wonderment, *But you're all so unorganised — until you begin to play!* The band's team spirit and co-ordinated swing, without its keeping a tight rein on outstanding individuals, represented a new kind of freedom for him.

QJ: Yes. In Yugoslavia we had some of our most ethusiastic audiences. Perhaps they spoilt us for Athens which came after them.

RH: And Iran, Persia? How did you find it there?

QJ: Persia was very, very crude. It was still like five hundred years ago there. The audiences were very warm though, once they caught on to what we were doing. When we arrived, we found they hadn't even heard of Louis Armstrong! We felt very close to them though, and to the people of Pakistan — mainly because of a link we found between the rhythms in their native music and the rhythms in ours.

RH: The USIS had made all the arrangements for the tour of course.

QJ: The lay-out of the tour made everything look good. We always had good hotels. But we all got 'Karachi tummy' when we were in Pakistan, and Charlie Persip went down so bad with it we had to use a Pakistani drummer part of the time.

RH: Marshall Stearns, reporting on the poverty that was everywhere the band played, mentioned you giving away a suit of clothes.

QJ: That was in Persia. Billy Mitchell and I bought a suit of clothes for a sailor — also shoes. The poor guy earned only $1,88 a month in the navy. When we told him how much an American sailor earned he wouldn't believe us. But everyone was poor in Persia it seemed. I remember, Ernie Wilkins's saxophone had been misplaced in New York, so when he reached Abadan he went out to borrow one. Wow! He found saxophone-players there who had used only one reed for more than a year!

RH: Were you able to do any arranging on the tour?

QJ: Ernie Wilkins was my room-mate after Syria, and we spent a lot of time together trying to force each other into writing. Phil Woods too. He was very interested in learning how to arrange. He's a very talented little cat.

RH: Dizzy arranged his *Tour De Force* for the band in Athens, which surprised me because he must have been kept continuously busy as diplomat extraordinary, meeting people and so on. Still, I can't think of a better choice for this than Dizzy with his brilliant natural showmanship.

QJ: Dizzy was always with cobras or camels or something. I expect you saw the famous photograph of him blowing the snake-charmer's pipe, and the snake draped around his neck. Well, I bought that pipe afterwards. I have it at home in New York. All kinds of native drums too. My apartment in New York has all sorts of souveniers from all over the world. It looks like an ancient-and-modern museum. My favourite piece though is the 45-degree angle trumpet which Dizzy gave me. It was his personal, gold-plated one.

H: Dizzy can clown, and yet, underneath it all, he manages to remain an idealist. As a man, as well as a musician. That incident in Ankara, when he refused to let the band play at a diplomatic garden-party unless the poor children crowding outside the walls were let in. That's typical of Dizzy. The band itself, of course, non-segregated, with black musicians and white musicians intermixed, was guaranteed to break through a lot of human barriers wasn't it?

QJ: Yes. Likewise Melba Liston, a glamorous trombonist playing publicly in countries where they were still using the veil. But we certainly couldn't understand why the people in the streets of Pakistan were segregated — because they all looked the same colour to us!

RH: That would be the caste system. Something far more difficult to break down than the colour bar.

QJ: I got slapped by a performing monkey in a Pakistani street. Had a scar on my forehead for a week. I couldn't get a reputable antiseptic, so I had to keep putting shaving-lotion on it — and didn't it sting!

RH: After the tour, and once the band had returned to New York, you went into Norman Granz's studio, and recorded almost the entire concert programme at one freewheeling session. Most of the time with first 'takes'. I know that these recordings, the 'World Statesman' and half the 'Dizzy In Greece' albums, have been criticised on account of imperfect balances, some internal ones, too, but I feel that by letting the session run as freely as a concert the engineers caught something of the band's real-life spontaneity, something of the spirit of its public playing. The men knew the scores well — and to have insisted on continual re-takes might have taken the edge off this spirit. Might have made the performances sound mechanised. Did you feel the same way at the time of the sessions?

QJ: No. I was disappointed with the session, and having to record seventeen numbers in two hours, *all* first takes and with no one there in the control room to supervise the session. I think re-takes would have improved these particular recordings without spoiling the band's spirit.

RH: Well, I remember your own *Jessica's Day*, always an interesting score for me, with the small-group ensemble set within the larger ensemble was one of those performances. Immediately after the Granz session didn't Benny Golson at last come into the band?

QJ: Yes. Benny joined the band prior to its leaving for South America. As soon as he joined he wrote *Stablemates, Whisper Not* and several other wonderful things for Dizzy — and on tenor-saxophone he played the end!

Benny was the only change for the South American tour, after Ernie Wilkins had dropped out. I was out of the band for a while when we got back from the Middle East. I had some writing to do, and as the band was playing theatres, playing only two or three tunes at each show, the library wasn't really marred by a change of personnel. Reunald Jones, Jr — son of Basie's former lead man — deputised for me then. I knew the South American tour was coming up though, and while I was out of the band I'd play a little trumpet at home each day to keep my chops in order.

RH: Where did the South American tour take you?

QJ: Quito, Ecuador — Guayaquil, Ecuador — Buenos Aires, Argentina — Montevideo, Uruguay — Rio De Janeiro, Brazil — Sao Paulo and Bella Horizonte, Brazil. Again flying all the way. I met Villa-Lobos, the composer, in Rio. Benny Golson, Father Crowley and myself all went to his house one afternoon. A profound individual and composer.

RH: That meant you passed through several zones of climate. Did this affect your playing, or were they with you all the way?

QJ: No to the last. Exactly the opposite. The climate was all against us. In the Middle East it had been hot as hell, but hadn't interfered with our playing. In the South Americas it was winter — and as cold as a whore's heart. In Quito we caught hell at an altitude of 5,000 feet. Bad intonation and bad breathing on account on the rarefied atmosphere. Dizzy was smart and let Joe Gordon show off on all the trumpet solos. Joe almost killed himself. He was really ill after the concert, and had to drop out of the band. In Buenos Aires we used a trumpet-player called Franco Corvini, but after that we made do with the four trumpets.

RH: One last point, Quincy. Did you, on either one of the tours come up against any difficulty on account of language?

QJ: No. No language problems at all. Our music acted like an international language, and people everywhere accepted us on account of it. I picked up about twenty words of each language though, and was really confused at the end of the two tours!

Quincy left the band after the South American tour. 'I could've gone on balling with Dizzy, but I had writing to do and I wanted to spend some time with my family,' he explains.

Already too he had received an award — voted *New Star Arranger* of 1956 in the 'Encyclopedia Of Jazz' poll — although this now seems smallish by comparison with everything showered upon him since then.

Soon after this came the call from Creed Taylor, the record producer at ABC Paramount. Was Quincy ready to make a big band LP of his own jazz works? 'The day after Creed called I started planning the parts for my 'This Is How I Feel About Jazz' album'.

In the notes he made concerning this, his finest writing so far (and today recognised as another jazz classic), Quincy outlined his continuing attitude towards composing and arranging. 'This is,' he wrote, 'an attempt on my part to supply the settings, select the proper cast and musically portray my feelings about some of the less cerebral and more vital and/or basic elements contained in jazz. Trying to put into words the essense of these elements has made me realise that jazz is much easier to play than to say.

'At a recent Newport Jazz Festival,' he continues, 'one of the topics for panel discussion was 'The Future Of Jazz'. As a member of the panel I stated my preference again for 'a natural growth' instead of a forced or blueprinted development. Because of lack of time to explain this point thoroughly, it could possibly have been assumed that I was unaware of the possibilities uncovered only by *advancement* of jazz techniques. Such an assumption would be clarified, I hope, after a hearing of this album, as it has given me ample opportunity to present some of my favourite musicians and soloists in settings conducive to swinging and to their unlimited self-expression. (These latter elements comprise the most distinctive characteristics of jazz. Original voices are created and not mapped out, meaning you can't make a racehorse out of a mule.)'

Quincy contributed six scores in all to 'This Is How I Feel About Jazz'. When I heard the record through later, I was convinced that, not since Benny Carter, had there been a jazz arranger so naturally matured at or by the tender age of twenty-four. So, a jazz Mozart?

Each of his qualities had been uncorked like an essence and poured into the album: heart, warmth, vitality, humour (sometimes sophisticated, sometimes puckish), and always impeccable taste. Also musical efficiency, musical imagination, and the ability to fire an ensemble and its soloists, most of all rhythmically. Plus one other quality I tried to define when I reviewed the LP for *Jazz Monthly* ('Keepin' Up With Jonesy'). This was his being in line with the jazz tradition.

Beginning with a point Quincy had made in his own notes, I wrote: 'His arranging and composition, so different from the all-experimentalist writing, of say, Bill Russo, wishes to advance the known substances. In other words, to promote the music by what has been said already in jazz as a direct aid to saying newer things, and this without juxtaposing jazz and classical writing techniques or strange instrumental groupings in a self-conscious way. More than any other younger jazz inventor he seems able to appreciate what has happened in jazz so far as well as what he himself wants to happen.

'At the present time too many modern arrangers are only preaching about the importance of the tradition in jazz. Jones is prepared to practise what he preaches, and throughout this, his arranger's showcase, his finger never leaves the pulse of jazz past as well as jazz present. The six arrangements it contains, while concerned with men and music of the post-Minton's Playhouse years, are also in line with a grand tradition in jazz scoring — the tradition of Benny Carter, Don Redman, Fletcher Henderson, and even before that of Jelly-Roll Morton.'

Three of the six scores were Quincy's own compositions: *Stockholm Sweetnin'*, *Evening In Paris* and *Boo's Blues*. The remaining three were compositions he had been interested in for some time: *Walkin'*, originally popularised by Miles Davis and a blues straight out of the gutbucket, ('Guaranteed to strike a groove,' Quincy himself wrote. 'We tried to get the feeling of an informal session, using orchestral backgrounds written to sound like 'head arrangements' rather than complex lines. I think we took full advantage of our guarantee and retained a feeling of complete freedom and realisation.'); *Sermonette* by Julian 'Cannonball' Adderley and an instance of the spiritual's place in jazz ('As Dizzy used to say, "this feels like one of them good old good ones" — if you forget your rules of HIPology for a moment, I think you'll dig this tune. This is where a lot of the current jazz scene really came from. . .'); and finally *A Sleepin' Bee* by Harold Arlen, a song from the show *House Of Flowers*. This show, although not a commercial success on Broadway, was blessed with an Arlen score and lyrics by Truman Capote, the chameleon-like author of *Other Voices, Other Rooms* and who wrote the plot of *House Of Flowers* first as a short story in his collection 'Breakfast At Tiffanys'. Quince saw it and was captivated by the song and by Diahann Carroll's delivery of it. ('As usual, Harold Arlen's composition here is so harmonically complete, it leaves little need for composition within the melody,' he wrote).

Quincy gave considerable thought to astute programming as well as to purely aesthetic ideals in writing for the LP. In the set he had scores of varying texture and impact, performed by an orchestra of shifting proportions with a wide selection of soloists. There are some surprising finds too in the writings: the use of a baritone-sax as an anchor and with the flute on top, for instance, giving the ensemble a range of nearly five octaves, so effective in the big band pieces; the verve and economy of the brass parts in *Walkin'*, reminiscent of a head arrangement at its best; also the very relaxed pulse of this performance, sustained through nearly eleven minutes. Then there is the orchestration of Clifford Brown's original trumpet chorus during *Stockholm Sweetnin'*. This is particularly audacious. Every melodic turn Brownie improvised for the Swedish record has been used, even the little double-tempo and triple-tongued runs he used to link the main phrases. Cleverly grouping small units within the ensemble and frequently moving the lead from low-voiced to high-voiced instruments, and back again, Quincy effects an imaginative and at the same time respectfully sensitive orchestration of the chorus. The flute and double-bass alternating one bar *ad libbed* with one bar written to give an improvised feel to the opening of *A Sleepin' Bee*, and the phrases following, so richly voiced. Not least the atmosphere and impressionist sketch supporting the free-jazz tenor-saxophone on *Evening In Paris*, so deftly drawn. All these are typical of a Quincy Jones at his most enterprising.

Two extra points arise on account of the album. First, the way other musicians will go out of their way to play for Quince — and out of respect for his music. For instance, although there was not too much money to splash around, and because he had the key-role to play on *Evening In Paris*, tenorman Zoot Sims caught a plane from Washington DC just to make this one number. Again, one of the world's three greatest vibes-players, under contract elsewhere, appeared under the pseudonym 'Brother Soul'. Others who gained permission from their respective record companies to be on hand for the creation were Art Farmer, Jimmy Cleveland and bassist Charles Mingus.

The second point concerns Truman Capote and the use of *A Sleepin' Bee*. Even though he had no idea of it at the time — because the plot of the book had not yet reached its final *dénouement* then — Quincy was going to complete one of his major works by writing the music score for the film of Capote's *In Cold Blood*.

Shortly after the release of 'This Is How I Feel About Jazz' he signed to return to Paris as a staff arranger for Barclay Records. 'The atmosphere in Paris is so relaxed that it makes work easy,' he wrote me. 'How can I describe all I feel for this city? Life doesn't seem the rat race that it is in America and yet really you are working just as hard.'

He rented an apartment along the Boulevard Victor Hugo in Neuilly-sur-Seine. He thought he might spend six months of the year in Paris and the other six in New York.

Chapter 5

METAMORPHOSIS . . . AND
THE BIRTH OF A BAND

Ever since April 1919, when the Original Dixieland Jazz Band from New Orleans arrived in London via Chicago and New York, the bigger and lesser names of American jazz have been fascinated by Europe while Europe itself has remained fascinated with them. The reasons have varied, of course. Some musicians want to do a tour with *any* band as the means of sight-seeing their way around. On the other hand, the tenor-saxophone star Coleman Hawkins crossed the Atlantic in the 1930s because impresario Jack Hylton offered him a fat cat's salary to appear at the London Palladium. Hawk then decided he liked Europe so much that he teamed up with Benny Carter, the arranger and multi-instrumentalist, and toured around France and the Low Countries until near the outbreak of World War II. It was the ambience of Europe they appreciated, plus being away from all the hassles of the New York rat race, of scuffling after jobs and, not least, the colour prejudice. (The Social Revolution in the US was still years away.) Many jazzmen who were largely unappreciated in their own country suddenly found themselves heroes in Europe. They enjoyed the food, the hospitality, the enthusiasm of the audiences, and if you were black it no longer mattered.

Following World War II this drift across the Atlantic picked up again. After the 1949 Paris Jazz Fair tenorman Don Byas announced he would never return to the States; and he never has, eventually basing himself in Holland. James Moody stayed on too, while Sidney Bechet applied for naturalisation and married a Frenchwoman. Drummer Kenny Clarke now became a Paris resident; likewise Johnny Griffin and the octogenarian Benny Waters. Other soloists settled in other places: Benny Bailey and Sahib Shihab (the former Ed Gregory) in Stockholm, Dexter Gordon and Kenny Drew in Copenhagen. Even Stan Getz lived for a time in Denmark. And now the ubiquitous Gerry Mulligan spends part of each year in Italy, composing at a retreat in Milan. Moreover, all of these players have been helped by the tremendously improved standards of their European rhythm sections.

Quincy Jones's sojourn in Europe has to be viewed from a different standpoint, however. Partly it stemmed from the frustrations of his current situation in New York, partly it involved a need to broaden his horizons, to go on with the search. He accepted the fact that music is a never ending development. Nevertheless he himself was feeling incomplete. Nor had he fully recovered from the shock of losing Clifford Brown in that turnpike accident of 26 June 1956. Clifford, still only twenty-five when he died, was for Quincy the most important trumpet soloist since Dizzy Gillespie.

Quince had been getting enough work in New York, but it was commercial work, not many jazz gigs. He did manage to land one superb writing assignment featuring the altoist Sonny Stitt. This occurred in September/ October 1955 for Roost Records, Inc. (LP 2204). Stitt, long regarded as the inheritor and natural guardian of Charlie Parker's be-bop style on alto-saxophone was not appreciated as an interpreter (and at times invigorator) of beautiful ballads until this time. Quincy more than compensated for this with the surrounds he provided for Sonny on *My Funny Valentine, Come Rain Or Come Shine, Love Walked In*, Tadd Damron's *If You Coul See Me Now, Stardust* and *Lover*. Although allowed only a small backing group (three trumpets, trombone, tenor and baritone saxophones, plus rhythm) his scores are both brooding and intuitive, and Sonny Stitt as soloist took every advantage of them. The set also included a Jones original *Quince* — a loping, almost Basie-like theme with an attractive contribution from trumpet/cornetist Thad Jones.

Otherwise, though, Quincy considered popular music in America did not seem to know where it ought to be heading. This was, of course, before the Dizzy Gillespie 'World Statesman' tour, and Quincy was writing for Ray Anthony, sometimes Tommy Dorsey, and filling in with Rhythm & Blues dates. But as regards straight 'pop', the Fender bass had arrived and there was an increasing use of improved amplified guitars — without the pop singers of the day being at all sure of how best to exploit them.

Already in his latest letter in 1957 to me Quincy had complained about 'Elvis Depresley' and of animals in films earning more than the actors. Now, as he later explained to Roberta Skopp of *Record World*, it had all of a sudden burgeoned.

'On Dorsey's show, I remember one summer was the first time anybody ever saw Presley. The guys in the band just wanted to die when he came up for the first time, because he couldn't sing in tempo. And so the band couldn't play with him. He was shakin' his butt all over the place and they had to send to Nashville to get some dudes to play with him because he couldn't understand time. And Tommy said, *Don't worry, we'll just get this over with, get it out of the way, and next week we won't have to worry about it anymore!* But he was wrong: we got in 4000 letters. I don't have to tell you the rest, Tommy never did get him off the show. . .

'At the time there was so strong a conflict because I was coming out of the Swing era and the last part of the be-bop revolution, the first modern jazz era — and there was a strong resistance to what was going on then.'

The resistance Quincy is speaking of here involved both musicians and public. 'The older musicians resisted be-bop so fast it was ridiculous. They didn't get into it at all, and half of them couldn't even play it. Also there was the artistry and the life-style. Billy Eckstine and Charlie Parker, Dizzy, Miles Davis, J.J. Johnson, Art Blakey — you name them — Gene Ammons, Leo Parker, Sarah Vaughan. That was the spawning ground for most of the predominant influences in modern jazz throughout the world today. That was truly the beginning. But in revolutionary music like that they forgot all about show-business and audiences; they couldn't have cared less; they were playing for themselves, to develop and give birth to a brand new music. But then the public let them off; the public couldn't handle it. And so that's why, I believe . . . we reverted, in the early fifties, probably to the worst era in music in America's history. I'm talking now about musical quality. I'm not talking about indentification, nostalgia and all that. I'm just talking about music. Because that was the dumbest music. Everybody who was in on the 1950s music will probably kill me for saying this now, but it really was . . . absolutely the dumbest music that you could remember of any decade in America.'

Roberta Skopp asked: 'Do you think that was because they couldn't deal with anything else at that time?'

'They didn't know anything about music,' Quincy responded, 'and they had just come out of what was probably the most progressive and complex era. I'm not saying whether that's good or bad in terms of an audience relating to it, but it was the dumbest music.'

So he hung on in New York but with the seeds of dissatisfaction all the time growing up within him. He carried out his studio jobs with professional diligence. Thanks to Marvin Holtzman he was in at the birth of Epic Records, a division of CBS Records; and naturally he was grateful to Creed Taylor for the ABC-Paramount opportunities ('This Is How I Feel About Jazz' and 'Quintessence').

'At Epic, the other arrangers were Don Costa and Ray Ellis. We did Johnny Ray, Chuck Willis, Big Maybelle. Then I started to write for Dinah Washington (Quincy's important introduction to Mercury Records). I did a lot of things with her. Arranging and doing some original songs too. She was wonderful to work with. She had the religious background, the blues, the band bit (with Lionel Hampton) and could handle the popular ballads and swingers. Also that voice — that earthy, intense quality.'

However he hardly ever touched the trumpet now — hence the problems which arose with his *embouchure* when the Dizzy 'World Statesman' project suddenly materialised. Again he recalled (wryly) another typical show-business story. 'I remember George Avakian in 1956 brought me an acetate of a track runner[1] he had found out in San Francisco who he said was going to be the biggest singer around — jazz singer that is — and I had the acetate around for a little while. It had standards on it like *Old Black Magic, Caravan*. And then Dizzy Gillespie called and started to talk about the desert and asked me to put the band together for the Middle East, etc. And so I had to give that demo back to Avakian at CBS and it turned out to be Johnny Mathis. And he was a jazz singer on his first album — before Mitch Miller took him upstairs — and when I came back all I could hear was *Twelfth Of Never* and *It's Not For Me To Say* and all that stuff!'

After the Middle East and before the South American tour Quince had played with Dizzy at The White House (for the Correspondents Association). 'And when we came back to Brazil on that SA trip Dizzy sat in with a rhythm section at the Hotel Gloria and just played straight be-bop over a Brazilian rhythm section. In the front row sat Antonio Carlos Jobim and Astrud Gilberto — they were just teenagers and I swear to this day that's where the *bossa nova* came from.'

But back in New York the scene seemed as sour as ever, and when the offer came from Barclay Records in France Quincy did not hesitate. 'I agreed to go for three months, maybe six, and stayed nearly three years.' It was from this time that I date his own particular metamorphosis.

Until now Quincy Jones had been a hungry arranger, and a gifted but occasional composer with some formal training and a largely jazz background. He knew the touring life of a band musician and he had accumulated some experience of writing for and conducting in the recording studios — the tough New York studios. But in Paris the opportunities were greater. His commercial work in New York had been determined by

---

[1] And a high jumper. He once held a California high-jump record.

45

very tight financial budgets. In Europe over this period the costs of hiring musicians and studios were appreciably lower. Also, although Eddie Barclay and his wife Nicole were running a straight commercial company, they wanted Quincy to tackle an extremely varied series of projects and let him have the resources he needed. 'As a jazz arranger in New York doing horns and everything, with just the be-bop and small commercial dates I could never get string sections or anything. It had become stereotyped and I wanted to write for strings. In Paris I could use 89 strings!'

In addition he began to see for himself how a successful recording company is run, how important sessions are planned, routined, booked for and otherwise organized. He observed the producer's relationship with his recording engineers; why the studio is laid out in a certain way, and how the subsequent edits are achieved. Quincy's eaglet eyes noted the different pieces of sophisticated equipment involved, such as the equalisers and the echo units, while at the same time he would be having after-hours *aperitifs* with the company's other excutives and learning about the value and methods of publicity and salesmanship. He picked up on every trick — and remembered everything important.

Meanwhile he was also continuing his own music studies, and with none other than Nadia Boulanger. She, easily the most revered music teacher in France, had been born in 1887 and won the coveted *Prix de Rome* at the Paris Conservatoire when aged twenty-one. She was only the second woman to do so. (The first was her elder sister Lili, who died at the age of twenty-four leaving two symphonies and a number of unperformed choral works.) The friend amongst others of Ravel, Poulenc, Darius Milhaud and Olivier Messiaen, Nadia Boulanger set severe standards for those pupils she agreed to take. On the other hand, like the cellist Paul Tortelier, if the talent was obvious and the pupil poor she would teach for free. With all her notable gifts she was humane, and a brilliant communicator. Years later, at the age of eighty-eight, for a *Los Angeles Times* calendar she joked that, since 1904, in a life given over to the love of teaching music, her two most distinguished pupils had been Igor Stravinsky and Quincy Jones. Quincy himself said of her at this time: 'She's truly fantastic. She seems to know everything that's ever happened in music. And she's so quick. In a single session she'll sort out writing problems that have been bugging me for years. Also she's showing me how to use vocal groups in other ways than just accompanying a single voice.' (An early portent of The Wattsline?)

He was studying every day with an obsession typical of him when working. He was meeting and talking music with Olivier Messiaen. But he remained stubbornly his own man. As David Burnett James points out in

Ravel, His Life And Times[2]: 'Too many pupils end up as little more than ciphers of those they study with; and that is why many artists, whatever their *genre* may chance to be, become disillusioned with teaching. . .' But this never happened with Quincy. What Nadia Boulanger and Messiaen gave him was an increased ability to be himself.

He scarcely ever took time off. In the afternoons and often through the night he would be arranging for Barclay. He estimates he wrote something like 250 recording dates for them. Also, while in Europe, he wrote orchestrations for Charles Aznavour, Andy Williams, cemented what would become a longstanding relationship with Billy Eckstine, and finally recorded with Sarah Vaughan, 'The Divine Sarah'. Afterwards Roy Berry, the English publisher of such song hits as *South Of The Border* and Ray Noble's *The Very Thought Of You* and *The Touch Of Your Lips*, asked Quince a $64,000 question: 'How do you relate the vital differences between the truly outstanding artists, say, Ella Fitzgerald and Sarah Vaughan? How is it possible?' Quincy sat silently sipping his tea for what seemed like a full five minutes. Then he replied with immense deliberation. 'It isn't possible. But I think of it like this: Ella is *the* instrument; Sarah is *the* voice. But also there is still Miss Peggy Lee to be considered. . .' Eventually he would get to conduct for all three.

One other, almost a maverick recording event occurred when Quincy decided to pay a return visit to Stockholm, and conduct a session there with Harry Arnold's Radio Studio Orchestra. 'Man, this city reminds me so much of Clifford Brown I feel haunted,' he remarked gloomily upon arrival as his taxi took him through the darkened streets. But the following morning his attitude had changed and the occasion was high with excitement, especially when Quincy renewed his friendships with Benny Bailey, Arne Domnerus and Bengt Hallberg.

Obviously in a career covering over a thousand recordings it is difficult to detail all of them. Also this one, 'Quincy's Home Again!', for Swedish Metronome is hard to come by, but it's no less important for being that. The band plays with a verve and a soaring *élan* which even the best of American groups would find hard to better. And they had Quincy there in front of them.

Not long before this I had been bemoaning the fact to Quincy that, on a Ted Heath single I had produced called *Swinging Shepherd Blues*, there was a wrong note played within the final chord. It made a chord that still sounded right but was not as per score. And nobody had spotted it until

---

[2]Midas Books/The Baton Press, 1984.

the disc was released and actually in the charts. 'Listen, man,' he stressed. 'Nothing's ever perfect-perfect. And in any case if they haven't bought the record by that stage then they're not going to. It's like working at your running order for an LP. If you're unlucky enough to end up with a real dog then it goes track five side two.'

A similar thing happened during the Harry Arnold recording of Horace Silver's *Room 608* which Quincy had arranged. During the playback somebody put his finger on a minor error and suggested another take. 'Look,' Quincy replied firmly, 'you always have to sacrifice something. One of the trumpet players might hit a bad one or forget a certain way of phrasing but actually it doesn't mean too much. The main thing is that the feel is there, that the thing has spirit. This take is crazy!' They also recorded Silver's *Doodlin'*, the Basie-style *Count 'Em* (originally written for a Jimmy Cleveland date) and *Meet Benny Bailey*, which starts softly with the minor theme played in unison by Bailey's muted trumpet and Rolf Blomquist on flute. Benny then switches to some virile open horn and there is a screaming climax. But pride of place on the album clearly belongs to Quincy's *The Midnight Sun Never Sets*, the beautiful ballad he composed in Paris with the singer Henri Salvador. 'Arne Domnerus brought tears to my eyes with this,' Quincy remarked after the session.

When he mailed me a finished copy of the record he signed the back 'To Raymond. Mon petit pote (chum). Long may you make me write letters. Love. Quince.' But alas for me, though fortunately for him, the long and detailed letters would become hurried notes and sometimes just telephone messages. He was entering a period when, as regards work, his feet hardly ever touched the ground:

'I paid a flying visit to New York and John Hammond fixed for me to meet the producer of a new Broadway show with Pearl Bailey and Al Nicholas, etc. And this sounded fabulous because they wanted me to arrange the score, get my own band — I mean cream band, and I had the cream, too — go to Europe with the show which was about 70 people — and break the show in, in Holland, Belgium and France and then meet Sammy Davis, Jr in London and work the show three weeks there and come back to Broadway and open for two years. Now this was a perfect way for us to start the big band too, and have the band together all the time. They were to be paid very high salaries so I got Clark Terry from Duke Ellington's orchestra, and Jimmy Cleveland, Quentin Jackson, Phil Woods, everybody I wanted.'

As if this assignment was not enough, once back home Quincy was given the opportunity of composing and arranging a whole album for Count

Basie — not the kind of offer to treat lightly. He got down to writing the Basie LP 'One More Time' while continuing planning the birth of his own band. 'You can listen and listen and still you can't tell what they've got, these Basie men,' he said, shaking his head. 'What personalities!' But the record turned out to be one of Basie's best ever as regards the exploitation of his soloists' personalities. *For Lena and Lennie* (Horne and husband, of course) is the kind of slow, sensuous swinger tailor-made for trumpeter Joe Newman. *Rat Race* with its leap forward in time clearly suggests the booting, out-going tenor duet by Frank Foster and Billy Mitchell, while *The Big Walk* could only mean bassist Eddie Jones with the microphone wide open on his strings and taking on the rest of the band. Quincy borrowed back *Quince*, originally done for the Sonny Stitt LP as a feature for Frank Wess's flute, and *Jessica's Day* from the Gillespie book, and he allocated *The Midnight Sun Never Sets* to lead-alto Marshall Royal. *I Needs To Be Bee'd With* was a new, brilliant slow blues featuring the growling sounds of trombonist Al Grey, while with *Muttnik* Joe Newman's muted trumpet and Al Grey's more blustering trombone give the band a sound that goes right back to the Jones-Smith Incorporated group of 1936, the name Basie first recorded under — when Quincy was exactly three years old. But *Muttnik* also includes passages from *Keepin' Up With Jonesy* of 1953!

Throughout there is always the singularity of the Basie piano — economical as usual, never intrusive, but at the same time deeply felt. 'You can write for my band again any time you want,' he told Quincy afterwards. The words were to prove prophetic.

About the formation of his own band he sought the advice of Dizzy Gillespie who, over the years, has experienced every possible pitfall in trying to keep good groups together. Setting the show aside, Diz told him, 'You must have two other books on hand — one for dancers and one for concerts and clubs.' Judging from an article, 'Starting A Big Band', which Quincy then wrote for *The Jazz Review* that is what he intended to do. He also wrote a wise thing in the article about his human relations policy. *I had to have musicians who were men as well as creative . . . My men had to have good conception — not just a studio approach — but they also had to be good straight guys. One man with a dissonant personality can ruin a section, no matter how skilled a musician he is.* Dizzy Gillespie again: 'That's tied to another piece of advice I gave him. I told him to hire men who would put the job over friendship and be able to take direction. That's why it's often difficult to lead men with whom you once worked as a sideman in some other band. Another thing . . . is that the best way to keep a band sharp is to keep getting it new music. That keeps them in shape.'

In the meantime Irving Green of Mercury Records had offered Quincy a recording contract for the new group — which resulted in 'The Birth Of A Band' LP, still available in catalogues around the world and one of the most admired big band albums of all time. Quincy certainly called for and got the cream in the make-up of his own first regular big band. In the trumpets were Clark Terry, the iron-man Ernie Royal on lead, Joe Newman and himself; for trombones Jimmy Cleveland, Urbie Green, Quentin Jackson and, remembering their Gillespie days, the delicious Melba Liston. For saxes he had Phil Woods, Frank Wess, Benny Golson, Zoot Sims and Sahib Shihab. The rhythm section was Patricia Anne Brown (piano), Milt Hinton (bass) and another ex-Ellingtonian, Sam Woodyard, on drums.

One or two other arrangers were brought in to help with the intensive recording schedule. Al Cohn came in to score Lester Young's *Tickletoe*, Melba Liston the unlikely *Gypsy* which featured Phil Woods, while Benny Golson contributed *Whisper Not* and (somewhat reluctantly) parted with *I Remember Clifford* to Nat Pierce — a superbly proportioned and evocative ballad featuring Clark Terry on flugelhorn. Quincy wrote the opening, *The Birth Of A Band* and co-wrote *A Change Of Pace* with Harry Arnold. He also had the honour of Harry 'Sweets' Edison on trumpet and Sam 'The Man' Taylor joining in as guest artists for the exciting closer, *Tuxedo Junction*.

All in all the LP gave the new band a tremendous send-off, and Bill Basie agreed to write the LP sleeve-notes, concluding 'I wish Quincy my best and only regret he hasn't room for another piano player in his band.'

However, if the LP turned out to be a triumph, the projected show, 'Free And Easy' turned into something less. 'We put the band together first because the guys had to be on stage in costume and this was before 'No Strings'! No music in the pit. Just like hustlers and pimps — playing cards and everything. We got to Belgium, Holland and got to Paris and the plan was fine so far, but the Algerian crisis came up and then we never got Sammy Davis, Jr. The show closed — they said tomorrow night the show's over and guaranteed us transportation home. So I called up my agent in New York and said, "Hey, man they pulled the tablecloths from under us, what do we do?" He said: "I'll get you back all right later." But then it's a month later. And I'm still in Europe. And now there's no guaranteed transportation home and I'm looking at all these people, the big band plus their wives and children and dogs and everything. What followed was probably the most beautiful experience and the largest nightmare I ever

50

had in my life. We were in every country in Europe, no agent, no manager and just life's vagabonds — no money. But I had to pay them $4,800 every week. It was just incredible! And I mean these weren't guys who were working around, who'd been hanging out for years, they were top musicians.

'I had to call everybody I knew in Europe and do any kind of thing we could get going, just to keep everything afloat, you know. And that lost us months! So we leave Paris and I go to Sweden, I know a cat up there, and he said, "I have three gigs for you and there was a guy back in Paris who said "I'll get some gigs together for you." So he books us on sixteen one-nighters. We go to Sweden, then get back in town (Paris) and the dude is gone with a guarantee for all our sixteen one-nighters, just disappeared and we have no jobs. But we have to keep that money coming in every week. So I hocked the publishing interests on all my copyrights and got my people back on the SS *United States*. This was at the end of 1960.

'The band stayed loyal. When we got back we played at Basin Street East with Peggy Lee, with Billy Eckstine and then Johnny Ray. But I was just too sick, too tired, I couldn't handle it. And I was flat broke.'

Chapter 6

MISTER GREEN STEPS IN

Rescue came in the unlikely, imposing form of Irving Green, the President of Mercury Records Inc. Green, with the reputation of a tough operator and a very skilled negotiator, nevertheless was first and foremost a music man and a natural spotter of talent. He had had his eye on Quincy since 1957 and those successful sessions with Dinah Washington. Which in turn had prompted him to take a chance over recording Quince's big band. 'Those charts you did for Dinah were just great,' he told him, immediately giving the young man a psychological lift. '*They Didn't Believe Me, Makin' Whoopee, I'll Close My Eyes* and that original you wrote for her, *You're Crying* — all absolutely fine. Also 'The Queen' liked working with you. The way you surrounded her special kind of phrasing so skilfully. . .

'And of course I loved 'The Birth Of A Band' LP. Forget the show's failure. They come and go on Broadway all the time. But good bands don't come that often. In other words, what I'm suggesting is you work for us here at Mercury. Partly as a staff arranger. You can pick up with 'The Queen'. But also as an artist and repertoire man, looking for and producing new talent.' Quincy caught his breath. 'You can pay off all your debts,' Green went on,' and I'll teach you what the business side is really about.'

'So I decided I'd better go back to school with Irving,' Quince said. 'He taught me everything. And two years later he made me a vice-president of the company — and I was doing 250,000 miles a year travelling. He taught me about pressing plants, mergers, the whole bit.'

Mercury Records and its subdivision, Emarcy, were soundly based financially and now had affiliations with the powerful Philips company of Europe — and this meant that I next saw Quincey in London doing a running, jumping, standing act. But he was fit and keen and looked remarkably happy with life. 'We were doing 250 albums again each year and it was an administrative gig. Irving was cool though and knew all that was going on. Some of the cats kept saying I was just a be-bopper and too idealistic to know what the commercial side was about. But Irving let me keep my band together for when concerts came along, and then I found that demo by Lesley Gore. . . .'

Just before linking with Mercury on a permanent basis Quincy had achieved a longstanding ambition when he scored the major part of an album for ABC Paramount (another Creed Taylor production) featuring his old chum, Ray Charles. During the years between, with several hit records, but above all, *What'd I Say?* Charles had become the hottest property in international blues singing. Quincy was thrilled to be invited into the project. He arranged for the album ('Genius + Soul = Jazz') Charles's *From The Heart* which also features Ray's trumpet discovery Phillip Guilbeau. Likewise Bobby Timmons's *Moanin'* and the rocking *One Mint Julep*. But the outstanding item on the album is *I'm Gonna Move To The Outskirts Of Town*, a blues virtually unsung since the great Jimmy Rushing version with Basie of 1942. Charles plays the Hammond organ on this track and in one passage becomes so overcome with emotion that he sobs over the music. Clark Terry on trumpet makes a superb contribution and Phillip Guilbeau supplies a fine obligato. The 'soul' part, needless to say, is never in doubt.

QJ: 'Ray Charles used to say, if you just deal with the pure soul of all music, everything from the schottisches to blues, it'll come out right. What a musician he is. He's even taught me to read music in braille!'

In seven years at Mercury Quincy gave up playing the trumpet completely. But under Irving Green he gained enormous experience of the record industry and show-business generally. He was young and eager and Irving liked his style. He taught 'Q', as he now became nicknamed, about administration, office routine, artists relations, how to handle difficult agents, how records are cut and mastered — and most importantly he encouraged Quincy's potential skills as a record producer. It was at Green's urging that he produced the first Julian 'Cannonball' Adderley LP, and eventually a session with Oscar Peterson.

The Jones big band continued to record with Mercury and to make occasional appearances on the concert platform and at festivals including, notably, the Newport Jazz Festival of 1961. But Quincy was finding that in his new capacity as a record executive, he had less and less time for composing or arranging. He had followed up 'The Birth Of A Band' LP with 'Golden Boy', then an album devoted to the musical themes of Henry Mancini, but on 'The Great Wide World Of Quincy Jones' which followed, he only conducts the band. The scores are by Ernie Wilkins (*Lester Leaps In, Ghana, Everybody's Blues* and *Cherokee*), Al Cohn (*Air Mail Special, They Say It's Wonderful*), Ralph Burns (*Chant Of The Weed*) and Bill Potts (*Caravan, Eesom* and *I Never Has Seen Snow*, yet another contact with Truman Capote's writing.)

On the other hand he began to receive more awards. He received his first 'Grammy' from NARAS in 1963; in 1964, in Holland, he received the Thomas Edison award at the Grand Gala du Disque. And he came to be increasingly in demand as an arranger and producer for singers. He continued to work for Dinah Washington until her sudden tragic death in Detroit in 1963, by which time Sarah Vaughan had also signed with Mercury (likewise Billy Eckstine). Ella Fitzgerald also became interested in Quincy's writing; and by 1961 so had Miss Peggy Lee. Quincy scored two Capitol LPs for her, one using a big band backing and hardline standards and blues, the other an altogether different, dreamier approach with strings, French horns and ballads.

Irving Green was tolerant about Quincy taking other, occasional prestige jobs and justifiably so since, before long, he gave Mercury one of the biggest successes in the company's history. The demonstration record of the bright and breezy Lesley Gore led on to her becoming a winner who won ten gold discs, each one representing a million singles sales with LP follow-ups. Probably the best-known of these today are *It's My Party, Judy's Turn To Cry* and *You Don't Own Me*.

Lesley Gore was not a jazz singer, but she was pretty, vivacious and exactly what many clean-cut American teenagers were looking for as an antidote to the bumps and grinds of Presley & Co. Quincy Jones surrounded her with just the right kind of commercial arrangements, which suited both her personality and the songs she sang.

Perhaps by now, though, it was time for Quincy to start making changes. He continued to be deluged with arranging offers: to write for Helen Merrill, LaVern Baker, Aretha Franklin, Sarah Vaughan again and, on the male side, Johnny Mathis (how things can come full circle!), Paul Simon, Bill Cosby, Milt Jackson, Tony Bennett, B B King, Jose Feliciano, Bill Withers, Billy Preston et al. He managed to cope with most assignments. But he was never at home. His marriage was collapsing. He felt there had to be something else.

Then, quite unexpectedly, he received a telephone offer which no American arranger could conceivably turn down. Was he prepared to score, conduct for the LP, and afterwards go on a nationwide tour with Frank Sinatra and the complete Count Basie orchestra? This was in 1964 and the recording sessions were set for June in Los Angeles. Even Irving Green could not object. In any case Quince had done Mercury proud; especially with Lesley Gore.

So he locked himself away and, once again, began putting pen to paper for very long hours.

In the absence of his particular *bêtes noires* (i.e. certain pressmen and other, obvious hangers-on) Frank Sinatra can be as considerate and generous a man as one is ever likely to meet. For example, that outstanding actor, the late Lee J. Cobb, could hardly speak of him without getting a lump in his throat. Lee had been divorced, then suffered a bad heart attack and felt that his whole career was finished. 'Nonsense!' was Sinatra's reaction. He took Lee into his own home, got him the best medical care and nursed him back to full health. Afterwards the actor went on to triumph in such films as *On The Waterfront* and *Twelve Angry Men*.

Also Quincy Jones tells a story of how, one Christmas, it looked as if Frank Sinatra's mother might be left on her own. Immediately her son had her flown out to the Palm Springs house, waited on her all over the holiday and even hired a 12-piece choir to sing her favourite carols. . . .

However, musically, amongst fellow professionals, Sinatra is supreme — hence his nickname 'The Governor'. At recording sessions he is on-going and workmanlike, an easy man who knows exactly what he has to do and does it. Contrary to popular misconception he does not arrive at a recording session surrounded by heavyweights. Nor does he rewrite that stale press idea of his alcoholic consumption. Out of a case of Jack Daniels (Bourbon) delivered beforehand, only two shots — drowned in ice and water — are gone by the end. The other bottles are given away to members of the recording team.

Sinatra has an acute ear and does not shun self-criticism. He has good pitch, and if it goes off slightly he detects it immediately and wastes no more time on that take. Or he will stop in mid-take and make his own selection of a likely editing-point, thereby not only conserving everyone else's energies, but ensuring his own best possible performance by the time the number is finished.

Sinatra now took to his new arranger as easily as he had done previously to the piano-playing Count from Red Bank. Quincy Jones meanwhile was burning both the midnight oil and the breakfast eggs to get the work done. Interspersed sometimes with, as he once described it to his friend Gerry Mulligan, 'that rolling about underneath the piano syndrome'. Yes, even Quincy has the occasional mental block! But enthusiasm provided the momentum. It was a commercial project, of course; but he was writing for the top singer in America, using some of the finest songs ever composed and aided and abetted by the most polished, swinging big band in the world. (In fact, a band so well-rehearsed by Basie's deputy and lead-altoist Marshall Royal that if a player made even the smallest error every head would turn round on him, while guitarist Freddie Green — custodian of the Basie rhythm section — used to travel with a stick to poke drummer Sonny Payne in the ribs if the latter showed any sign of racing the tempo.) The record producer was Sonny Burke, the recording engineer Lowell Frank. Harry 'Sweets' Edison, long a favourite of Sinatra's, rejoined Basie for these sessions to bring the trumpets up to six and the trombones were augmented to five. They also added a vibraharp (Emil Richards) and then, for the second and third sessions, sixteen strings. On 9 June they kicked off with *The Best Is Yet To Come,* Sinatra as usual right on form from the outset, and they finished on 12 June with *Wives And Lovers.*

Frank pronounced himself delighted with the album, 'It Might As Well Be Swing', and even more so when one of its tracks, *Fly Me To The Moon* gained him more royalties and airplay than any other single he had released in years. He said he would like, other commitments permitting, to keep this special triptych of Basie, Jones and himself going. And Frank being Frank he naturally did — leading on via isolated separate performances to the sensational 'live' double-album released from their concert at The Sands, Las Vegas, in 1972.

You can picture the scenes at Vegas just by listening to the records.

Every occasion such as this is a big one for Sinatra. His professionalism is never to be doubted. He talks scarcely at all during the morning, stops smoking, has a steam-bath in the afternoon. Then half an hour before going on stage he will have a final run through with his regular accompanist Bill Miller before slipping into his tailored tuxedo, still warm from the valet's attentions. Meanwhile out front the atmosphere is electric. Sitting at the nearest tables there is a veritable 'Who's Who' of show-business — Rosalind Russell, Yul Brynner, Mike Romanoff, Judy Garland. A paunchy businessman waves a handful of $10 bills at a suffering headwaiter, hoping to get a better seat. 'I couldn't get you a better one for $10,000', comes the reply. It all reminds one of Dean Martin's fond remark: 'It's Frank's world, we're just lucky to be living in it!'

Eventually the house lights dim, the stage comes alive and Basie's Sonny Payne is twirling his drumsticks ready to go. Basie, 'Mister Cool', short and squat at his Steinway signals *One O'Clock Jump* and the ten-minute 'warm up' is under way. Just ten minutes, but based on forty years of musical experience and ending with the rousing *All Of Me*.

Next, silently, unobtrusively, a young man, short and elegant, walks on and adjusts his music-stand in front of the Basie men: Quincy Jones. This is the signal for pandemonium, the biggest burst of audience applause heard in Vegas for years, for within seconds the spotlights are switched on, the superstar has bounced into view, the band swings and songs are flowing from that familiar, much-loved voice. Great songs: *Come Fly With Me, I've Got A Crush On You, I've Got You Under My Skin* (and how Basie and Quince drive the band with this one!), Johnny Mandel's *The Shadow Of Your Smile* (from *The Sand Piper* film), *Street Of Dreams, Fly Me To The Moon* (again), *You Make Me Feel So Young, Get Me To The Church On Time*, then *September Of My Years* and *It Was A Very Good Year* (two of the very best of Quincy's scores) followed by *Don't Worry About Me* and the haunting *Where Or When*.

While the Count and his Merry Men take time for tea, Frank is joined by Bill Miller, a thin, grey-haired man, and who looks — according to sleeve-note writer Stan Cornyn — 'as if he hides under mushrooms to avoid the sun's rays'. But the star sings his celebrated bar-room ballad *One For My Baby And One For The Road* and then Matt Dennis's beautiful *Angel Eyes* and the silence throughout the packed room is gold of the 22-carat variety.

In fact Frank does not take a break but elects to have some tea and a napkin delivered to him on stage so that he can regale the audience with a selection of his latest anecdotes. My favourites are those wishing luck to the punters. 'Basie and I haven't been having too good a week,' he explains. 'First we went up to see the Grand Canyon and found it was closed. Then we decided to invest in a pumpkin — only to be told they've cancelled Halloween. . .'

With Basie and Quincy back on, the tempo hots up again and the show drives on to its ecstatic conclusion — ending, inevitably, with *My Kind Of Town, Chicago Is*. Which, in fact, Frank does twice. Or rather he breaks the performance in two, inserting a few nice words about this often-maligned city, before building up to an amazingly roaring climax.

What a night!

But after a triumph with Frank Sinatra, where does one go next? You just can't collect Sinatras like oil moguls buy Rolls-Royces or build bigger palaces. No: after the 'It Might As Well Be Swing' LP there had to be something different. Which is not really surprising. After painting his *La Gioconda* Leonardo worked on the designs for a submarine. Renaissance Man again.

Happily, though, this was not to be the end of the Sinatra/Jones connection.

Chapter 7

INSIDE CELLULOID CITY

Quincy, or 'Q' as he was now increasingly often referred to, had been a film 'buff' from as far back as he could remember. 'Everything, man,' he had said to me in London at our first meeting, 'from Buster Keaton and Laurel and Hardy to *Casablanca* and then the epics, Cecil B De Mille — the whole bit. . .' Bobby Tucker took off his spectacles and smiled. 'Quince, baby, one day you're going to be right in there writing those soundtracks,' he prophesied.

So: after a long hard slog at Mercury and on other recording projects Quincy decided to try his luck, put his toe in and test the Hollywood water. He knew about the terrifying power struggles at all levels within the major studios; the sort that are portrayed in Nathanael West's *The Day of the Locust*. Nevertheless, he shared the popular fascination with being involved in the whole process of film-making. Besides, his increasing work with artists of such stature as Peggy Lee, and especially Frank Sinatra, persuaded him not only that he might like living on the West Coast, but that that might help to give him the *entrée*.

To begin with, however, there was one big difficulty. He was black. Not that prior to this there had been any particular problem about black artists *appearing* in feature films, if they suited the plot or had their own special popularity. From Rex Ingram, and the famous 'Rochester' who, notably with Jack Benny, specialised in grinning chauffeur or butler roles, via big musical stars such as Paul Robeson and Lena Horne all the way through to the more recent dramatic parts played by Sidney Poitier, Hollywood has had its usual keen eye for potential box-office talent. Also it has made films essentially for the large black urban sections of the population. Duke Ellington and others benefitted from these in the early days.

But several other areas of movie-making had remained exclusively white — production, direction, scriptwriting — and including significantly, the musical soundtracks. Amongst the latter there had been black incursions occasionally, most notably by Benny Carter who got his *Blue Mountain* theme into the film of Ernest Hemingway's *The Snows Of Kilimanjaro*. Later he wrote for Alfred Hitchcock, as well as the musical scores for *A Man Called Adam* (1966) and *Buck And The Preacher* (1972). Otherwise the major assignments, and consequently the most lucrative ones, stayed firmly in white hands, especially those of less than a dozen men, including Alex North, Miklós Rózsa, Alfred Newman and the amazing, extravagant Dmitri Tiomkin. On one occasion Tiomkin conducted one of his scores in London, and was asked — with some hesitation — by a specialist soloist he had hired whether a fee of seventy pounds would be in order. 'No', he snapped back. 'Charge two hundred. If you don't, back in Hollywood they'll think you're no bloody good!'

However Quincy Jones is both brave and extremely persevering. Also he had a genuine white sponsor in his composer friend Henry Mancini. In the end he won out, becoming the most famous black musician in Hollywood's history and, coincidentally, gaining affluence together with another cascade of prizes, nominations and awards. At the same time his success opened the doors of the film and TV studios to other gifted black composer/arrangers — such as Oliver Nelson, Benny Golson and J.J. Johnson.

On a purely personal level, though — and much more important than a big house in the Brentwood section of Los Angeles, the blue Mercedes and the swimming-pool — going to the West Coast resulted in Quincy making a thoroughly happy love relationship. His first marriage had collapsed under the stress and strain of touring while working and living in the East; so had his second to a Swedish girl. But in Hollywood he met Peggy Lipton, a blonde ex-model now turned actress and frequently seen on TV, who transformed his life. Of Peggy, Quincy still says, 'She's my greatest source of inspiration. She's smart, compassionate, imaginative, creative, she writes music and stories, and she never hassles me.' To begin with, they didn't even think about getting married. 'It's just a word,' was Quincy's opinion. 'It's conditional with or without paper. It's like the word jazz. What kind of jazz? If people can be friends, that's a start. People get all hung up. Don't let any hostility build up. If she snores at night or you don't like your mother-in-law, say so!'

Another bonus of his move West was a close association with Dave Grusin, the keyboards and synthesizer expert. Originally from Colorado, Grusin settled in Los Angeles during 1962 and, after he met Quincy, the two became major influences upon each other. For, just as in his recording career Quincy made it his business to learn everything he could about the backroom aspects, so when he got to the West Coast he did the same with the technical side of music for films. In order to hold the glamour spot with the baton, he reasoned, one needed to understand all that was possible, whether in the editing rooms or simply how to use a click-track or a movieola. You don't need to have all the aids involved all of the time; but it is vital to be alert to what is there.

Consequently Grusin was exactly the kind of man at this point to fascinate him, largely because, apart from his composing and being a fine piano-player, he is also a wizard when it comes to electrified music-making. The particular significance of this was to re-emerge when — years later — Quincy had given up films and gone back into the recording studios.

Finally, the uses of success and affluence were rounded off by Quincy's business conduct. Much more experienced in the aftermath of Paris and Mercury, he was able to channel the rewards of the film world into projects of his own, music publishing, a production company, promotion, even the development of new artists.

In return, what Quincy gave to films and TV was unique, even if it was not always appreciated. In effect, what he gave Hollywood was an overdue musical spring-clean. Before him, nearly everything emerging from the established composer/arrangers (Mancini excepted) sounded either complacent or it had varicose veins. A lot of the composers no longer bothered to do their own orchestration. Indeed many good new productions were marred by inferior scraping and blowing in the background. No doubt directors and others on the visual side should be made to take much of the blame for this. To all but a handful of them only two kinds of music seemed to exist, — 'romantic' and 'grand' — with instructions issued to the composers accordingly.

When Quincy arrived on the scene, therefore, it must have looked to half of them as if this was a creature come from Mars. No more cloying strings or pompous fanfares in his writing. With his background of soul, blues, jazz and pop, plus his wider orchestral studies in Boston or with Nadia Boulanger, his big band experience, his ability to compose catchy themes and above all his vigour, these were precisely the characteristics he proceeded to feature in his scores, to the astonishment of many of the old hands. But then, to their double astonishment, his scores were accepted with increasing delight by the public. Following this, music in the movies was never to be quite the same again.

Quincy had had some small experience of film work when he became involved in a low-budget Swedish production, *The Boy In The Tree,* starring Arne Sucksdorff. Also, there was his own natural enthusiasm. 'By the time I was 15, I'd read the back off Frank Skinner's book on film music, *Underscore,*' he says. 'And I'd sit in a theatre and close my eyes and identify what studio a film came from, just from the style of the film's score.' But it required patience — which usually meant nibbling away at the edges (and fairly modest edges) of TV, and filling in meanwhile by writing more vocal accompaniments.

The breakthrough came — or so he thought — when he landed the job of writing a full-length score for *The Pawnbroker,* starring Rod Steiger. (Henry Mancini reported: 'They 'phoned me, the producers, and said, Look, we know he's gifted. But he's also black. So will he be reliable?') Although not typical of a lot of his later film music, on account of the sombre, haunted nature of the plot, Quincy's orchestral scoring is nevertheless fully sensitive to the unhappy 'broker's turn of mind and his memories of Nazi Europe'. The film proved an enormous success with the critics and it won Steiger an Academy Award for Best Actor. Given the doom-laden subject matter the box-office was less impressed, and in traditional Hollywood fashion, everyone associated with an unprofitable film suffered. Quincy had to improvise his working efforts for a year before he was given his next feature film.

This one was for Universal. Entitled *Mirage,* it starred Gregory Peck, and Quincy had his first real taste of the old-style film industry's lack of imagination when it came to the music. 'The producer was scared to death that I was going to write a blues in the main title,' he moaned. With good reason. Although consciously made as an 'entertainment' film, and despite Peck's normally guaranteed success, *Mirage* too failed with the public. Another year passed.

But Quincy didn't give up. 'Even so, I was nervous,' he admits. 'With those long breaks between pictures, I said to myself, *I just don't know if I can wait that long between meals.*'

The really big, genuine break then occurred when somewhat luckily he got the assignment at Paramount to write *The Slender Thread,* starring Sidney Poitier and Anne Bancroft, quickly followed by *Walk Don't Run* for Columbia, with Cary Grant and Samantha Eggar. Poitier's popularity with the public was peaking by now and both films did well. Quincy's contributions, despite what seemed to old hands their unorthodoxy, were an acknowledged part of the success. And Hollywood rewards success. Afterwards, and for the remainder of his years in full-time writing for the screen he had all the big films and major TV shows that one man could handle, even a hyperactive one.

The cream of the crop? In this writer's opinion, *Enter Laughing* for Columbia with José Ferrer; the excellent *In The Heat Of The Night* for Mirisch with Rod Steiger and Sidney Poitier again; *In Cold Blood* for Columbia (see page 64); *The Italian Job* for Paramount with Michael Caine, Noel Coward at his best and including a real romp of a Quincy music score, especially when it accompanies the famous car chase; *John And Mary* for 20th-Century Fox with Dustin Hoffman and Mia Farrow; *Cactus Flower* for Columbia with superb performances by Ingrid Bergman and Walter Matthau; *They Call Me Mister Tibbs* for Mirisch, again with Poitier; *The Anderson Tapes* for Columbia with Sean Connery, and Quincy having an electrical sounds field day; *The Hot Rock* (sometimes known as *How To Steal A Diamond*) for 20th Century Fox with Robert Redford and George Segal . . . this soundtrack is surely underrated, being both jokey and groovy as well as prominently featuring Gerry Mulligan's sax solos; *The New Centurions* for Columbia with George C. Scott; and of course *The Getaway* for National General with Steve McQueen and Ali McGraw. [1]

On TV Quincy is probably best-known world-wide for his *Ironside* theme, used throughout the series that featured Raymond Burr as a wheelchair-bound Californian chief detective. As with so many of Jones's melodic ideas, it is a case of once or twice heard, then never forgotten. But the theme is also atmospheric, with the evocation of a police siren preceding its main (flute-based) melodic line, and heavy brass bursts which suggest the violence to come. However, Quincy was so swamped with work at this period that he imported Oliver Nelson to score the remaining incidental music for *Ironside*.

Otherwise his TV work has proved remarkably varied, if in Quincy's case predictably so. As examples: *The Wide World Of Entertainment Roasts Redd Foxx* (ABC); *Sanford And Son*, again with Foxx (NBC); *Hey! Landlord* featuring Sandy Baron and Will Hutchins (NBC) and of course *The Bill Cosby Show* for NBC and *The New Bill Cosby Show* for CBS. Both of the latter incorporated another memorable Jones theme-tune, *Hikky-Burr*. Next one must contrast such all-out laughter vehicles with the devotional tribute programme *Duke Ellington . . . We Love You Madly!* of 1973, a CBS special; with *Roots*, or with *Rebop*, a clever children's educational show which, incidentally, includes the bright and bouncy, *You've Got To Do It Yourself*. He even moved into the sphere of animated

---

[1] See Appendix for the complete list.

TV, chiefly with the ecologists John and Faith Hubley, a partnership which resulted in *Eggs, Of Men And Demons* and *Dig*.

The feature film *In Cold Blood*, however, is regarded by many — rightly, I believe — as his masterpiece in film music. It was a project he regarded as of the utmost importance, one which renewed his connections with the author, Truman Capote, as well as introducing him to the skilled director Richard Brooks. Later Quincy commented: 'It was one of the few occasions where the composer of the film's music and the producer of the film were totally attuned as to what should be done with the picture. He [Brooks] was so involved . . . that when I suggested he add special sound equipment to theatres so as not to lose any of the intricacies of the music, that's exactly what he did. As a result, the music did for the picture what I'd intended it to do. It was an integral part of the characters' minds and their motivation, not just background for the action.' He added, 'It was real. Richard Brooks is a thorough cat. He got into the psychology, you know, what makes minds like that (the two murderers). It was one mesmerising experience. And it really happened.'

Capote's book, which he began to research shortly after the crime was committed, concerns the particularly brutal murders of an isolated, but fairly well-heeled Kansas farming family, the Clutters, by two young men, Perry Smith (played in the film by Robert Blake) and Dick Hickock (Scott Wilson). But Herbert, head of the Clutter family, believed in banks and cheques and the murderers escaped from the house with only a fistful of dollars. Unfortunately then, because they had had no previous involvements with the family and for a time skipped to Mexico, it took Detective Dewey years, first of all to identify them and next to catch up with them. Capote stuck with Dewey and his quest through all of these years — and eventually he was present at their long-delayed executions. He described the resulting book as 'a non-fiction novel' and of all his books it is his most impressive contribution to modern literature.

In approaching so daunting a project Quincy realised that, as with *The Pawnbroker*, he had to forget almost entirely the groovy, and soul, and other styles with which he had previously shaken up Hollywood. Except in a few spots, he needed to rely upon his orchestral training (Schillinger, Boulanger, Messiaen) and then his own imagination. The result is masterly — while its integration with Brooks's visuals, and his direction of the actors, is often uncanny.

Quincy handles his materials and the large orchestral forces with consummate artistry, and what is composed is always sharply appropriate to the film's story and atmosphere. The main title music, for example, is not

Quincy Jones aged 20. *Melody Maker*

Ray Charles. *Melody Maker*

Lionel Hampton. *JVC*

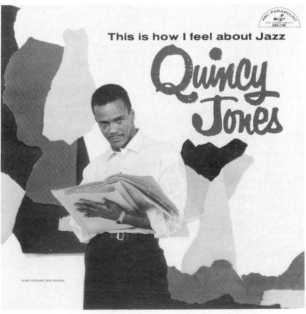

'This is how I feel about Jazz'. *ABC-Paramount*

Billy Eckstine. *Melody Maker*

Frank Sinatra and Count Basie. *Reprise Records*

Quincy Jones. *A & M Records*

Music from the film score composed and conducted by
QUINCY JONES

TRUMAN CAPOTE'S
IN COLD BLOOD

RCA VICTOR

Written for the screen and directed by RICHARD BROOKS
A COLUMBIA PICTURES RELEASE / PANAVISION®

'In Cold Blood'. *RCA*

'Smackwater Jack'. *A & M Records*

Patti Austin. *WEA Records*

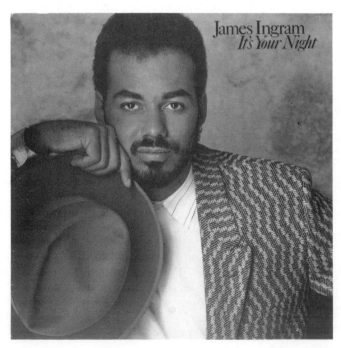

James Ingram. *WEA Records*

Quincy Jones with Michael Jackson and Steven
Spielberg. *Michael Jackson, Body and Soul* by Geoff
Brown (Virgin Books)

Quincy Jones. *Ebony*

Quincy Jones. *A & M Records*

just sinister, suggesting the evil to come; it is positively *chilling*, even more so, one might say, than *Scarbo* (The Devil) in Ravel's *Gaspard De La Nuit* or the second ('play with malice') movement of Walton's First Symphony. And yet this nerve-jangling opening, emphasised by its dramatic writing, is followed by a section of idyllic pastoral for strings as the camera reveals the distanceless golden wheatfields of Kansas — the area Capote called 'just out there'. We encounter the quiet, orderly life of the untroubled Clutter family plus their well-meaning but gossipy neighbours. Here, it is as though Vaughan Williams *à la* Quincy has temporarily taken over from the disturbing rhythms of *The Rite Of Spring*. However, this is short-lived and soon we are *Hangin' Paper*, back with Perry and Dick in their far from idyllic world. The music, briefly, is very groovy and hip (Ray Brown and other Quincy alumni are in the rhythm section); but, given their respective characters with their lack of moral responsibility, the violence is always latent. Perry was partly crippled and an aspirin-addict; Hickock was an obvious psychopath. Both were ex-convicts.

Once the two have settled on the Clutters as victims the darkness of the main title music returns, and stays, albeit this time largely via the percussion, and especially the double-bass. There are only three more moments of relief before the harshness of the inevitable climax. One, a lightening of Quincy's overall effect within the leitmotif that is *Perry's Theme*. (Perry Smith, although taking the lead in the break-in and subsequent killings had enough human compassion left to prevent Dick raping the Clutters' daughter.) Next comes *Lonely Bottles*, a blues which fits with a scene across the desert. Then, lastly, once the killers have arrived in Mexico, we hear a genuine night-club song, *Nina*, rendered by Gil Bernal. From here on the music accompanies further violence and eventually the judicial deaths.

So impressive did the score turn out to be that almost everyone predicted it must win the Academy Award for 1967. Unfortunately it was left out in the cold. After this, Quincy was to collect two more Oscar nominations, but only for the songs *For Love Of Ivy* from another Sidney Poitier film, and *The Eyes Of Love* from an indifferent movie called *Banned*, starring Robert Wagner. They too failed however, although the latter, an extra-sensitive ballad, has since become a favourite with musicians, most noticeably Oscar Peterson and Joe Pass.

Quincy, understandably, was disappointed not to clinch the award; and although he continued to score for major films up to and including *The Getaway* the seeds of his dissatisfaction seem to date from this point. Or, as he himself put it, 'This movie cycle started to get kind of grinding on me'.

Later, in an interview with Herb Nolan of *Down Beat*, he expressed his feelings at greater length. 'Hollywood and the movies are a fine workshop and a proving ground that you might never come across working on records. Just the idea of dramatic scenes; they force you into musical situations that one might never get into otherwise. It opens your head up. If you are writing for a record, be it three minutes or ten minutes, it has an organic unity that takes care of itself because it exists for the sake of the music. But in films, when you are playing outside of a scene, in a third dimension to create an atmosphere, you are dealing with a wholly different abstract form. The film dictates all the form to you. If you play music behind a murder, for example, and the film cuts to the next morning and total tranquillity in a different locality, you can get hung up on the sprockets and timing-key; in a minute and thirty seconds you have to get through with that murder and into neutral no matter how vicious you are . . .

'So there are frustrations. You have to deal with directors who don't know how to tell you what they want musically, or what they need. In movies you come in after there's dialogue, photography, interpretation, direction and lighting, so you are coming in with pre-established, pre-conceived dramatic direction. You can't fight it. The music is just one of the elements, which is hard to live with over a period of time. Now I'd rather deal with areas where I am thinking dramatically and musically, but the music is carrying the ball.'

Consequently when, in the fall of 1968, Creed Taylor asked Quincy to make an album for A & M Records, his first in four years, he jumped at the chance. 'I just wanted to see, get off on hearing the rhythm section groove with my favourite musicians. So it was just like a breath of fresh air to do that on record. And the tracks were all done within a week or so!'

'Walking In Space' proved to be a turning-point album, both musically and in its effect upon Quincy Jones's own thinking. From the opening of the title-track with Ray Brown's superbly rounded bass he takes the listener on a trip of varied moods, aided and abetted by the vocal effects of Valerie Simpson (her first time on record as a soloist), Freddie Hubbard (trumpet), Hubert Laws (flute) and the late Rahsaan Roland Kirk, who of course played most known instruments together with a few we did not know about.

A single released from the LP, *Killer Joe,* gained the most enormous airplay and in 1969 'Walking In Space' received a Grammy award for 'the best jazz performance by a large group'. It also received another Dutch Edison award.

Film and TV work would overlap with this for a time, naturally, but when Quincy's follow-up album, 'Gula Matari' in 1970, also won a Grammy for 'the best instrumental composition and best instrumental arrangement', he decided it was time once again to make records his principal concern. Records that is, and everything that flowed from them.

It is interesting, at this vital period, to tap how Quincy's mind was considering music itself. Further on in his discussion with Herb Nolan of *Down Beat* he says, 'I think of arranging as being very much like creating a watercolour painting. There are so many things that can be obtained from an orchestra in terms of colour. Adding colour to a composition is a trip I enjoy very much, and I am constantly exploring that orchestrally. It's like a painting or a tapestry, and with all the things available it's a pretty large canvas. But as you explore it, you find different ways to make the elements work. Take the soprano-sax, for example; if you have one of the top players like Jerome Richardson, who I think is better than anybody, you get more and more daring, constantly trying to bend that instrument into another orchestral context — another focus. There are also a lot of subliminal things that I think are very useful in creating colour, like doubling woodwinds on top or using lows to add reinforcement, bringing about synthetic mixtures. The Fender Rhodes piano, played in the low register in octaves with the Fender bass is an interesting colour. These are things you discover all the time because the combinations are endless.

'I'm all for decategorising the different musical pigeonholes. I don't think any of us can live with it any more, because there are too many things that are good in *all* forms of music. Basically they are all related anyway — blues, jazz and gospel music, it's all the same thing. I can't imagine people detached from one or the other. It would be like someone in gospel music hating jazz or *vice versa*.'

In fact what Quincy Jones hates in music is this very labelling; and the stigma which is sometimes attached to jazz. 'It's the word that struggles. The music isn't struggling, it's omnipresent — it's all over the place. It is just that *word*. I think the growth potential for jazz is endless, which is probably a reflection of the players involved. Most of the good jazz players I know keep their minds and ears open all the time for everything from Schoenberg to Delta Mississippi blues.

'The media has created a terrible negligence in terms of supporting different musical forms. The problem is that because of economics, or whatever is the basis for the motivation, they neglect the responsibility of tying together all the roots of the music they make their money on. It is a very strange animal because early American musical influences like the blues are still prevalent, and they are the main influence on everything in the charts today. It isn't obsolete, it's more alive today than ever. The blues travel right from the beginning straight through Billie Holiday, Prez, Charlie Parker, Coltrane, whatever. Until the pop field catches up with it all, which I think could take a long time, you're not going to be able to go any further. You know, because of the media imbalance, there are an awful lot of black kids who don't know about their own music, and it's very important that they understand it. It's tragic. I am very concerned, and I'll do everything possible to correct it.'

And good modern arranging?

'Maybe it's a question of sensitivity, perception and taste. After that you get into more specific things, like the flexible harmonic sense. For example, if a guy falls in love with clusters of 12-tone music, that doesn't mean he has to use it behind a blues singer all the time.'

Finally, it is an ironic footnote to his Hollywood and film years that, just as Quincy was making preparations for the momentous 'Smackwater Jack' and preparing to quit Hollywood except as a place to live, the committee which had previously rejected his work three times, should now invite him to arrange the music and conduct for the forty-third annual Academy Awards presentation ceremony!

Chapter 8

SMACKWATER JACK

'What's it all about anyway if you're not humble enough to share yourself with somebody else?'

QUINCY JONES

Quincy Jones erupted out back into the record industry, and a world of public appearances, firing on all cylinders. Lack of energy has never been one of his shortcomings. Moreover it soon became clear that his music and methods of making music had changed — and that he contemplated still further changes.

As to the music itself, modern jazz remained, together with all its earlier roots, especially the blues, but it was now augmented by elements of pop, rock, Rhythm & Blues, the soul sounds coming out of Detroit, new gospel singing, vocal groups and not least an adventurous development of electrified instruments and sound units. Quincy moulded each of these into a more than satisfying whole which, with subtle variations, and some less subtle, has become identified with him since about 1970.

This change and its stylistic manifestations have had their detractors of course, especially the increased use of amplification and its relevant spin-offs. But Quincy is swift to defend these. 'I hear the pros and cons,' he says, 'with some people complaining that electronics are going to replace the saxophone and others that electronic sounds bother them. Naturally I can't agree with these purists at all. For me, electronics are just another instrument in the orchestra, like an extra clarinet player. It's another tone or colour. Naturally you have to use it like garlic salt. You just can't slam it all around the place. But then . . . I prefer not to handle the purists. I can't help what they say. I just have to go with the hum — whatever hums to you and feels good. I listen to what is going on but I really don't care what choices I have. If something moves me emotionally and I feel like recording it, then I do it. The only thing you can trust is that little voice that hums inside you, and when it hums loud you have to respond. That's what it's all about.'

He could have added that the one feature of his music which has not changed is its strong rhythmic pulsation.

Meanwhile, in turning his back on films, Quincy was determined to take a firmer grip on his own career. Partly this meant his business affairs and building them up, but it involved also becoming a record producer again: initially, to safeguard what he himself might be doing, later as a service which he could extend to other artists.

The interesting point here is that few musicians have made good producers while they are still active in their normal playing or conducting capacities. Many have tried, but the difficulty is to stand back and think in a strictly objective way about your personal work and, for that matter, to take criticism. Also, it's difficult to keep an eye on what is happening in the control-box while you yourself are running things on the floor of the studio. In Quincy's case, though, there has been no particular problem. He had been trained at Mercury and, since 1971 when he clambered back into the driving-seat (musicians' slang for the role of the producer), he has not missed one traffic-light.

'Smackwater Jack', apart from being one of the outstanding LPs of its decade, is the fulcrum for all of this, the record which levered the various changes and the rethinking towards the kind of music we associate with the name of Quincy Jones today. As the late Ralph J. Gleason wrote, 'What he [Quincy] has done is to bring it all together . . . into just plain music. And even though we all know that music is music, it sometimes takes an event such as this to sum it up for us. The direct line of progression from Robert Johnson's Delta blues to the music of today's electric guitars at The Fillmore, the free flowing improvisations of Charlie Parker to the dynamic sounds of Blood, Sweat and Tears, and from the early messages of the intinerant blues singers to the sophisticated communication of the urban ghetto songs of Marvin Gaye.' He refers to the cross-fertilisation going on in contemporary music, and concludes: 'There have been many attempts in recent times to produce and make an amalgam of jazz and contemporary pop music. It hasn't always worked, mostly because the people involved in it really had their hearts in one place or the other. But where Quincy's heart is, there's always music and its perfectly obvious that he is at home in the language in all its dialects and that when he takes a current pop song, brings it to some jazz players and writes the arrangement for them to play, the result is music that has roots in all of

American music history but which is no hybrid music at all, simply a new thing.'

The album was recorded at A & R Studios in New York City. Quincy wrote all of the arrangements apart from *Theme* from *The Anderson Tapes*, a part of which he farmed out to Marty Paich. On the production side he had assistance from bassist Ray Brown and the overseeing engineer, Phil Ramone. Also the band was a large one — and impressive. Among the trumpets doubling flugelhorns, for instance, with Ernie Royal playing lead, Quincy had no less than Snooky Young, Marvin Stamm, Joe Newman, Buddy Childers and Freddie Hubbard. The trombones were two tenors and two basses; the saxes were mixed with a flute. Less expected additions were Toots Thielmans's harmonica and in the rhythm section organ, electric harpsichord, Moog synthesizer, Fender Rhodes piano, Fender piano, Tack piano, vibes, electric guitars, Fender bass, drums (the redoubtable Grady Tate) and two percussion. Harry Lookovsky led the violins.

The other surprising feature of the LP is how different in character each individual track appears when it is contrasted with its neighbour or neighbours. Treat them as a cohesive whole though and the result is unmistakeably Quincy Jones.

The title-song by Goffin and King was originally written with a decidedly Southern flavour. A frustrated young man takes a shotgun to the local congregation. 'On the whole it was another good year for the undertaker.' But here is no longer just a Country & Western story-song. It has become under Q's direction a gutsy blues with Sonny Terry-style harmonica and drummer Tate criss-crossing the beat in exciting fashion. Suddenly, Quincy himself pops up to take the solo vocal backed by a decidedly Tamla Motown-sounding vocal group. In contrast, Vince Guaraldi's *Cast Your Fate To The Wind* is altogether without words and starts out as if it is going to be a brass chorale with just a gentle rhythmic feeling — before the inspired, extrovert, leaping solos by Eric Gayle (electric guitar), Bobby Scott (piano) and Marvin Stamm (fluegelhorn).

Again, *Ironside* is still 'Ironside' to begin with; but only until Grady Tate switches to a straight fast 4/4 and Freddie Hubbard cuts loose, closely followed by Hubert Laws on flute and several brass blaze-ups which I never remember hearing in the TV episodes. And so it proceeds. Quincy returns as a vocalist to duet with Valerie Simpson as the introduction to a ten-minute version of Marvin Gaye's *What's Going On*. Freddie Hubbard flies right off the top register of the flugelhorn and Toots Thielmans whistles (humanly); while all the time the rhythm pounds along and the massed brass provides the punctuations. Guitarist Jim Hall then decides to be thoughtful, followed by an amazing electrified violin solo by Harry Lookovsky, be-bop style, based on a harmonica idea by Thielmans. Next it is the moment to turn the record over.

Theme from *The Anderson Tapes* is also predictable in its scored statements, but certainly not in the improvised passages, especially by 'Brother Soul' Milt Jackson (vibes) and the irrepressible Hubbard. While further contrasts occur as Belgian Toots Thielmans plays Ray Brown's *Brown Ballad* so delicately on harmonica and Bill Cosby adds his particular brand of laughter to *Hikky-Burr*. Lastly there is Quincy's *Guitar Blues Odyssey: From Roots To Fruits*, a focal history of the *genre* come to life and showcasing the assorted talents of four great players of the instrumnt — Eric Gayle, Jim Hall, Toots Thielmans and Joe Beck. It is nothing less than an abbreviated *tour de force* and provides the album with a most fitting climax. To quote Ralph J. Gleason once more: 'The late Charlie Christian was the man who made the guitar a solo voice in pop music and who first saw the possibilities of electronic amplification. He died so young, after such a short career that many young guitarists today who may have been influenced by him have no conscious knowledge at all of who he was or what he did. This composition places him right smack dab in the middle of the history of the guitar, from Robert Johnson to Jimi Hendrix and that's where he belongs. Such an extraordinary historical composition is an added bonus on an album that is so full of goodies that you can start anywhere and go in any direction with it because it's always entrancing. That takes the kind of love music brings out quicker than any other art.'

'Smackwater Jack' duly, and deservedly, won the Grammy award in 1972 for 'the best instrumental pop, rock or folk performance'. Quincy quickly followed it with 'You've Got It Bad, Girl', or what he calls his 'Sunday Afternoon' album because of its softer melodies and easier rhythmic feeling. It includes two Stevie Wonder compositons, *Superstition* and *You've Got It Bad, Girl*, plus Quince's own themes from *Sanford And Son* and *The Getaway* and his song *The Eyes Of Love*. However, the most popular item of the collection turned out to be *Summer In The City*, the first track. Originally it had been a group hit for The Lovin' Spoonful in the 1960s. Q says of his arrangement that he had decided to bring the song 'uptown' and give his feeling of summer in the black part of the city. Anyway, when it was taken off the LP and released as a single it gained him a further Grammy in 1973 for 'the best instrumental arrangement'.

In the meantime before this LP, but coinciding with some of the preparations for and the making of 'Smackwater Jack', Quincy had been progressing an idea based on what he called 'my recurring dream over twenty years'. This was the ambitious *Black Requiem*, a vocal and orchestral work that (musically) represented the struggles of black people in the United States 'from day one of the slave trip, out of the slave trip and into the compensation, the reality of it, what was really going on, then into passive resistance, the militant thing, and finally an era of hope. . .'

He himself is no militant; his life and the people he mixes with have caused him to be multi-racialist. On the other hand, he is acutely aware of his background and, on his travels or given the opportunity to read, his quest for further knowledge remains unabated. As he says, 'I have spent an enormous part of my career studying, researching, and attempting to trace the history of black music in the world today and the importance that our music has had on society as well as the music of the world.'

The research, he estimates, has led him through over three thousand books and as many recordings. No matter, he says, 'It is particularly interesting to note that with virtually every social trauma that has occurred, the face of music has been altered, sometimes drastically. It's also interesting to discover that European classical music was greatly influenced by the music of Africa and later Black America, and *vice versa*. It was almost like a relay team in which the Europeans borrowed heavily from our melodic lines. Naturally, both schools of thought embellished what they borrowed with their own sense of feeling — or soul, as I choose to call it.'

Black Requiem, as with its totally dissimilar stablemate 'Smackwater Jack', came to fruition in 1971. The much-praised performance featured Ray Charles ('friend of friends'), the Houston Symphony Orchestra and an eighty-voice choir. 'Quincy sacred and secular, both in the same year!' I could not resist thinking.'

He was bursting again with fresh ideas. Immediately afterwards he announced plans to develop the theme of *Black Requiem* into a total musical anthology for his next A & M album but one; probably a double-album, running to eighty minutes of composition. He would take the telephone off, corner himself in his music-room and do it. He wanted a narration by the venerable actor Ossie Davis (a San Fransisco abolitionist of the 1960s) which, coupled with his scores, would chart the development of black culture through to the present.

Then there were his hopes of producing a musical film, 'Mammy Pleasants'. It would have as its central core the musician's point of view, not the writer's, impresario's or actor's angle. 'Lots of people in the States have heard of Mammy Pleasants (also of San Fransisco). It's one helluva tale. Obviously I'm not going to rap out the whole storyline right now.

Let's just say she was a uniquely talented black version of Moll Flanders, Mata Hari and Joan of Arc. Some character, huh? And she had a most unusual way of fulfilling her missions.'

He also announced wanting to compose a Broadway musical — and to get his big band together for a concert tour of Japan, going on to China and then behind the Iron Curtain into Russia.

As it happened, other things intervened. During this period only the tour of Japan took place, briefly, in 1973. Nevertheless, as he stresses, 'It's that constant need to create and move that keeps me going. I get up at six and go on permanently non-stop until midnight, with occasional meal-breaks if there's time. It'll continue until one day I'm stopped. I could never imagine myself not working. Because my work is a labour of love, totally. If one day my love for it all starts to wear thin, then maybe I'll decide to hang it up — but, believe me, I doubt that time will ever come. . .'

By 1972–3 he was heavily into PUSH (People United to Save Humanity) or Black EXPO, an annual event sponsored by the black business communities of America. *Down Beat's* Herb Nolan tracked Quincy down to the huge Chicago Amphitheater, site of rodeos, sporting events, rock concerts and not least the infamous 1968 Democratic Convention when Mayor Daley's bully-boy cops effectively scuttled Vice-President Hubert Humphrey's chances of defeating Richard Nixon. It was at almost 7.30 pm, less than two hours before he was due on, and Quincy was still working with the musicians and testing the sound system. Everything had to be right for this multi-act show, topped this year by the appearance of superstar Roberta Flack.

'I've been doing EXPO for the past four years,' he told Nolan. 'It's something I think about all year round. We keep in touch with the Reverend Jesse Jackson (head of PUSH), and it's become a kind of family affair. Like with Roberta this year, we'll talk about different ideas, how to present things, whether to add strings, and what kind of band to use. Everybody is emotionally hung up in it and involved in the show . . . the preparation never really stops.'

After putting the finishing touches to his rehearsal, he then moved off the stage and into a growing backstage crowd where people demanded to shake hands, ask questions, wish him well and take photographs of him. He had to get back to his hotel, pick up his suit, then return and work out the final details with Roberta. But Quince still had a word for everyone.

By the time he got back to the Amphitheater the backstage activity was at full stretch. Jesse Jackson had arrived, the early acts were in progress and more photographers were at work. The musicians in Quincy's full orchestra (including strings) were gathering and likewise personalities of varying importance. Nolan remembers Isaac 'Shaft' Hayes sitting almost unnoticed in the corner of a people-swollen room.

Quincy's return pushed the excitement up another notch as everybody wanted a small piece of his attention.

'Reaching the questionable privacy of a makeshift dressing-room,' Nolan continues, '(an arrangement of curtains with his name on a piece of paper pinned to the outside), Quincy stopped long enough to answer questions and try to explain why he and his music have become so successful.'

'I live in the present time, always the present time,' he replied, with no hesitation. 'That way you're not involved with things you've already gone through; your experiences still count, but you are not hung up with getting stuck in a bag. The music we're involved in reflects every social, political and life-style shift and it changes from minute to minute. So if you worry more about living rather than trying to keep up with everything that is musically happening, the music will take itself right there. You don't have to sit around and think about it, it just happens if you leave your soul and mind open.'

By 1973 he had brought his experiences of both life and music into the formation of IBAM (Institute For Black-American Music) and its attendant charity, Operation Breadbasket. The Reverend Jesse Jackson again headed the committee. Other members included Cannonball Adderley, Jerry Butler, Roland Wiggins, Alvin Batiste, Donald Byrd, Isaac Hayes, Grady Tate, Roberta Flack and Donny Hathaway. Their purpose was to join with social leaders in Chicago in organising a 'Black Arts Festival' to feature concerts and musical seminars headed by Roberta, or Quincy, or other well-known musicians involved with IBAM, proceeds for the week-long event going into the foundation of a natural art and music library for members of the black community.

It all comes down to education, Quincy believes — education and helping each other. In his own words, 'Black people are programmed into cell divisions. Then once you make it — forget the ghetto. Well, Jesse [Jackson] has opened our minds now. Look, in the long run we don't want any welfare problems. Let people have a social choice. They shouldn't be forced to live in a certain way because of the necessity. We've got to work together rather than individually. You don't have to be a superstar to be happy. Do your own thing, but create conditions for total freedom: freedom of Choice.'

He would like to educate the youth of the world with his concept of

75

music spawned by his involvement with IBAM. Which was why the committee, under the Reverend Jackson, decided — via Quincy — to pay tribute to some of the great men of jazz and led to the CBS special, *Duke Ellington . . . We Love You Madly!* of 1973. 'Louis Armstrong died before we could get the plans off the ground,' said Quincy. 'So we didn't wait for a postmortem memorial to Duke. We wanted to let everybody know how we felt about him, while he was still alive to enjoy it.'

In creating this TV special Quincy himself acted as composer/arranger, conductor, contractor, producer, and even at times sound technician. Assembled to help him were Peggy Lee, Sarah Vaughan, Roberta Flack and Aretha Franklin. Also Count Basie, Louis Bellson, Harry Carney, Sammy Davis Jr, Billy Eckstine and Joe Williams.

Everyone who saw it agreed that TV history was made that night.

Chapter 9

AFFAIRS OF THE HEAD

1974 was the year of 'Body Heat', gold, and also darkness.

Quincy threw himself into the preparations for a new LP with all his usual zest and ambition. He kept to a punishing schedule, and to doing most of the work at night. He styled himself 'The Phantom of Brentwood'. 'I can hear better at night,' he says. 'The phone doesn't ring — and friends stop by to give me encouragement. Aretha (Franklin), Roberta (Flack) and Ray (Brown) often take the after-midnight cruise up here. With friends like that I'd wait up all night.

'But the real reason I write and arrange at such weird hours is the psychological effect it has on being creative. After you get past a certain point, your subconscious mind comes out. It breaks through all your artistic fears and inhibitions. You start to dream while you're still awake, maybe it's what you would call hallucinating. If you weren't writing they'd probably put you away.'

He'll go three, sometimes four nights without sleep (five when he was working on the Duke Ellington project). His secret, he says, is self-discipline; he knows how to deny negative forces and control his own emotions. At the same time, as he explained to A J Morgan, he pushes all his senses to the nth degree, trying to be as perceptive as is humanly possible. He pays tribute to his friends as another viable source of inspiration. 'Basie, Eckstine, Billie Holiday, they all pulled me through. Similarly the Baptist preachers; they have the strongest overall control as regards the blues and so on. But really music is the kind of person you are. Every music has its own soul. There's only 12 notes every time and they have to be shaped up. Sort of like a physics trip.'

For 'Body Heat' he was determined to make further changes. This meant less of a big brassy sound and more concentration on the potentialities of vocal groups and the rhythm section. As he saw it, 'Since the age of

77

fourteen I've been an orchestral junkie — that was my roots. Musically as a conductor/arranger, I had to have 50 or 75 people on a date to get the sound that I wanted. After a period of evaluation I realised that throughout my career I had been more or less ignoring the power and dynamism inherent in the rhythm section. To me the rhythm section — guitar, bass, percussion, keyboards — is the backbone, the major thrust of the music, and the horns, etcetera, are supplementary to the basic rhythmic track. After the 'Bad Girl' album I felt it was time for me to explore other styles of music, and in doing so I wanted to use a smaller group.

Almost as a footnote he added: 'Logistics is the problem with big bands. But this band will grow and I'll get a big sound out of eleven. It's a combination of all that makes me feel good. My 'Bad Girl' I said was a Sunday Afternoon album. This one here will be Saturday Night. It's funky!' Also it meant the influence of Dave Grusin had reasserted itself.

Quincy's own favourite track on 'Body Heat' is *Soul Saga (Song Of The Buffalo Soldier)*. 'Hey, man, they'd sing as they went into battle. They were some bad dudes.' But there were other composers involved; young writers QJ had come across in the districts of Los Angeles, such as Leon Ware, who co-wrote the title-track with Quincy and also contributed the ballad *If I Ever Lose This Heaven*, which since its 'Body Heat' debut has been recorded by The Average White Band, Coke Escovedo, Nancy Wilson and many other artists. Likewise B. Ighner, contributor of *Everything Must Change* — which now became a classic pop song.

Prominent musicians involved included Herbie Hancock, Billy Preston, 'Wah Wah' Watson, Frank Rosolino and Bernard 'Pretty' Purdie. Among the singers, apart from Q himself, were heard Valerie Simpson, Minnie Riperton, Joe Greene and Al Jarreau.

The album lost its maker a number of his former jazz adherents but caused a sensation in the pop world and the record industry generally. A favourite with the nation's disc-jockeys, it raced to over a million sales in the United States alone (certified by the RIAA), giving Quincy his first gold disc and staying on in the top five of the US pop, jazz and soul charts for well over six months. It also brought him the Johnson Publications Award for 1974 and the *Down Beat* critics poll, both for the 'best arranger, composer and recording artist'. He was now as much a 'star'-name as many of the artists for whom he had previously scored the musical backgrounds.

During the summer of 1974 Quincy was like a champion surfer, successful atop one of the biggest Pacific rollers. Nothing, it seemed, could go wrong for him. He had felt tired in the course of making 'Body Heat', and experienced intermittent headaches; but he put it down to overwork.

Meanwhile his plans were going ahead to tour with a new orchestra, possibly world-wide. Then disaster hit him — a cerebral stroke.

'To begin with, the doctors told me that I was supposed to die, they had me signing papers so they would know what to do with my body, but I was determined . . . to live. If you don't want to live, it's very easy to go, but all I could think of was God, I'm not ready yet, please let me hold on!'

In fact it was more complicated than the average stroke. Quincy remembers a few of the initial details. 'They shaved my head and used indelible ink to mark off the area where the skull would be opened to reveal the brain. They dressed me in a fresh hospital gown and rolled me down the long corridors at Cedars-Sinai Medical Center in Los Angeles and into the operating-room. Before the anaesthesia was given, I looked around the room and it frightened me a bit though my mind was hazy from the drugs I'd been given and because part of my brain had been floating in blood for several days. The heart-monitoring machine with its lights and dials, the blood-pressure apparatus, the trays of surgical instruments — everything gleamed under the brightness of the floodlights overhead. The room seemed filled with people — doctors, nurses, technicians. Among them was a familiar face, that of Dr Elsie A Giorgi, the Italian woman doctor who had rushed to my home, diagnosed the illness immediately and who pulled me through until the major surgery(s) could be performed.

Charles L Saunders, of the magazine *Ebony*, was assigned to the story. This is what he wrote: 'Quincy and his wife Peggy were lazing in bed on an extremely warm August afternoon . . . when Q's brush with death occurred. Quincy had been talking. Suddenly he grew quiet. Peggy noticed that he had slumped on his pillow. His face was contorted in pain. An aneurysm — a bubble-like defect — in the carotid artery that supplies blood to the right side of Quincy's brain had ruptured, spilling blood at the base of his brain and searing him with the most excruciating pain. (The actor and Kung-fu champion Bruce Lee died from such a rupture, and actress Patricia Neal suffered brain dammage when an aneurysm burst in her brain in 1965.)'

Quincy can still recall the intensity of the pain. 'It felt like somebody had shot off the back of my head. I'd never felt anything like it in my life, and after a while it seemed as if I could actually hear and feel the blood sloshing around in there. It was like the life was actually leaking out of my body. I could feel death. I wasn't ready to go, but I could sense, just in a flash, what it would be like not being here. I began thinking about my youngest daughter who was just a baby and didn't even know me yet. *I just wasn't ready to go. . .*'

'Quincy's aneurysm,' Saunders continued, 'was caused by a weak spot in the wall of the artery. He was born with the defect, which is not uncommon; many persons are similarly born and live long lives without a hint of trouble or with nothing more than occasional headaches. For others, like Quincy, the years of having blood surge through the artery and constantly pound against the weak spot causes it to grow thinner and thinner and finally thin enough to either spring a 'slow leak' or explode violently, and usually fatally, in a 'blowout'. Aneurysms kill more than a third of their victims upon rupturing, but in Quincy's case the artery involved lay *against* the brain, not deep within it, and the aneurysm ruptured in a 'slow leak' instead of a 'blowout'. Tests needed in order to prepare his body for the ordeal . . . showed that Quincy could live several days without surgery, but they would show something else: he had a similar aneurysm on the other side of his brain — one potentially dangerous but not ready to tear. Within weeks, however, Quincy would have to undergo exactly the same surgery again.'

Concerning the two operations, he proved to be one of Dr Giorgi's favourite patients. She says she could have hugged him during his visits to her office for the various check-ups, 'very, very important to me and a lot of other people'. She all-but abandoned her exclusive Beverley Hills practice for weeks in order to supervise every detail of the efforts to save her patient's life. It was decided that, for the first operation, the surgical team would consist of Dr Marshall Grode (who performed brain surgery on singer Stevie Wonder after an auto crash in 1973) and Dr Milton D Heifetz, a famous neurosurgeon who devised the widely-used 'Heifetz Clip', a special metal fastener used to trap aneurysms and render them harmless. He is also widely-known for his book, *The Right To Die*.

To quote Charles L Saunders again: 'Massive doses of cortisone had been given to Quincy to (drastically) lower his blood pressure and reduce swelling of his brain so that the surgeons could perform the miracle of opening the human head and actually handling the brain. An incision was made in Quincy's throat and the carotid artery was clipped in order to reduce the flow of blood. Then an incision was made from above his right eye to a point well behind his right ear, and the scalp was pulled down. Holes were drilled in the skull, then a special saw used to remove a large semicircular piece of skull. The brain was revealed. Exercising extreme caution so as not to damage any brain tissue, the surgeon lifted the damaged artery — the rupture measured about an inch across — and began the repair. Special surgical techniques were used to strengthen the surrounding wall of the artery, and a 'Heifetz Clip' was put in place.

Finally a metal plate was used to cover the gaping hole in Quincy's head (the originally skull bone could not be used; it would never heal), and the scalp was sewn. The seven-and-a-half-hour operation was over, and it was a success. But less than three months later, Quincy would have to return to surgery and undergo the ordeal once again. This time Dr Grode and Dr Charles Carlton (he operated on Patricia Neal) would open the left side of Quincy's skull to repair the aneurysm that threatened to rupture there. Once again there would be no complications. He would survive in perfect shape.'

Quincy Jones himself responded: 'I did some research and learned that the odds against my coming through just *one* of those operations was something like 80 to 20. I also found out that maybe 90 per cent of all brain surgery patients suffer complications that can either kill them or leave them paralysed or blind or unable to talk or something like that. Just one slip of either one of the surgeon's knives — just maybe a millimetre — and I would have ended up as a 'vegetable' or I could have been dead. Right after they finished operating on me, they took a black physician in for the same operation and he died right there on the table. Man, you consider the odds and you think about how close you came to dying — on two occasions. You think about how the doctors sawed open your head *twice*, went in there *twice* with scalpels and metal clips and things and actually held part of your brain in their hands! You think about all that and you realize you're still here and able to move and think and write music and love your wife and kids and all the things you enjoy doing. You think about all that and you have to stand back, and look at your life and see if you've got your priorities right.

'A lot of people were praying for me, and God just wasn't ready for me yet. But you still have to fight to come through. The doctors told me they could do maybe 30 per cent of what it took for me to stick around, but the rest was up to me. I remember when I came out of the anaesthesia that second time and I wanted to jump out of bed and yell, *Wow! I made it again! I'm still here!* That's how great I felt about being alive. And when you feel like that, you've got to start looking at everything in a different light — much more different than you used to see things. You look at everything, even a blade of grass, and you realise you're really very insignificant in the scheme of things. You think about how the doctors can take your brain and fix it up and keep you living and how someone else can just walk up with a gun and blow your brains out. So you start looking at people, you start evaluating them, you start looking at life anew and loving it second by second because you realise how fragile it is. Love/Death. Now

I know what a real fine line there is between the two.'

It was also Charles L Saunders's observation that the desperate fight for survival brought about a toughening of character in other ways: 'Quincy is not any longer the softie he used to be — the easy-going, never-argue kind of man. For instance, he laughed when he told me the story about a run-in he'd had with someone shortly after the operations. *The guy said something I didn't like and I cursed him real good. He didn't expect to hear that from me, so he 'phoned my doctor and said, Hey! Did y'all leave some of this nigger's brain on the operating floor?*'.

Quincy: 'I haven't turned mean or anything like that, but I don't ever again intend to hold all my feelings inside and refuse to get things out into the open. There's no more *pretending* about anything. If I don't like somebody, then I'm not going to have anything to do with him. I'm going to do the things I like and I'll do them around the people I like. I don't care anymore about the non-essential, the phony, the b.s. things in life — money, fame, the big houses and cars. Man, when they had my head open none of that stuff meant *anything*, and ever since then some of my old values have been turned upside down.'

In fact, Quincy is still deeply into what he refers to as 'the people relationship thing'. He still exudes warmth and he is above all a very *tactile* person. But as he says, 'I've begun really looking at people, including my friends, and seeing how we deal with one another. Man, it's a shame some of us abuse somebody else when we get the slightest chance. Not long ago I went through one of those security checkpoints at an airport. I've got all this metal in my head, so the alarm went off. There was this 'brother' who was a security guard and I begin explaining about my operations and the metal plates and stuff. He'd probably read about it in Jet or something, but he had to show me how great he was, so he made me take off my hat so he could examine my head. He came down on me with something like, "Man, I don't see no metal up there." I was mad, but all I said was, "Fool, it ain't up under my hat, it's inside my head!" He finally let me go through.'

Saunders concludes: 'In addition to the problem he has at airport security checkpoints, Quincy also has to avoid going near microwave ovens. The metal plates could become hot and scorch his brain. He also cannot play high notes on his trumpet; the plates tend to resonate. "*And it sounds like an express train running through my head!*"'

Chapter 10

AFTERMATH

'The first noticeable after effects, I suppose, were occasional lapses of memory, and weakness, but I have overcome both rather rapidly. The hardest part of recovery for me was staying out of my studio, for I had never been away from my music or my creative workshop for so long.'

QUINCY JONES

However necessary, convalescence doesn't fit in easily with the scurrying brain of a person like Quincy Jones. So, over the enforced lying-in of Christmas 1974, he jammed an extra pillow behind his multi-stitched head and thought afresh about his most cherished project, the furthering and expansion of the ideas he had first broached in *Black Requiem*. He recognised it was a monumental task — nothing less than the tracing and documenting of the whole history of black music.

'When I was in junior high school in the mid-1940s,' he says, 'all they taught us of black history was that Booker T Washington founded the Tuskegee Institute and Dr George Washington was great with peanuts. Both of those men did giant things, but there were many, many other black people of accomplishment, ranging from the ones who broke their behinds building the dome of the US Capitol to the Chicago doctor who pioneered open heart surgery. Somehow those things got programmed out of the history books they gave me to study, and it got programmed out of films, TV and a lot of people's memories. Well, it seems to me that if there's one thing that black kids ought to now about and be proud of it's their musical-cultural heritage, but they don't know much about that either.'

His overall, long-term project has as its working title 'The Evolution Of Black Music', and he has made use of his various travels in the States, Europe, the West Indies, South America and Africa to collect recordings, scores, books and numerous interviews with black music experts towards its realisation. 'I have more than 600 recordings of African music, and I've traced the history of 34 African tribes and visited with black people and listened to their music in such places as Dahomey in West Africa and Bahia in Brazil. It took me six months just to trace the history of the drum, which has always been so important in Africa. Why am I so interested in this? Well, black people's music has been our *life force*, not just a spectator-performer kind of thing as it was in Europe. To Africans, life and sex and food and worship and music were all part of the same thing. It's much the same today with American blacks, although our music was transformed somewhat because it was under bondage so long. But still, we've retained many of the elements. Listen to Aretha Franklin sing *Amazing Grace*. She's got to be as passionate sexually as she is when she's into that song. The African thing is still there.'

His intention is still that 'Evolution' will trace black music back to around 500 AD — with the completed work taking several forms. 'First, to release a double, 80-minute album of recorded music. It will involve a gospel choir, symphony orchestra, big- and small-band jazz, dance and solo voice. Then there'll be 13 one-hour shows with music, dance and narration on educational television. There'll also be a feature movie with the best of the visual scenes — and a symphony orchestra again. I have to pass on whatever talent I have to some kids. We've really got to share everything we've gained musically with the young. . .'

He had thoughts of working on the project in New York with show producer Peter Long and with Billy Eckstine's son, Edward. Again though other events have intervened — although some of his ideas did eventually spill over on to the musical soundtrack of Alex Haley's *Roots*.

By February 1975, when his doctors pronounced Quincy fully recovered, A & M Records were getting impatient for a follow-up to 'Body Heat', which had been so highly successful. The composer/arranger duly produced 'Mellow Madness'. Once again he elected to work with a smallish band plus voices. His own new works were the title-track, then *Beautiful Black Girl* (based on a poem by the Watts Prophets) and an arrangement of the jazz standard *Bluesette*. But also included — significantly — were four songs by two of his newest musical acquaintances, George and Louis Johnson, playing guitars and bass respectively within this latest of his assembled bands. Of the items they contributed, one, *Is It Love That We're Missin'* very nearly didn't get recorded at all. George had told Quincy during the final session that he had this other number to sing over to him, but it could wait till after they had finished recording. Quincy said, *forget it, man, play it for me now*. The result was that *Is It Love That We're Missin'?* became the hit single from the album and won an award from the Hollywood Chapter of NAACP as 'the best single by a jazz artist in 1975'.

Meanwhile Quincy was so excited by the musical qualities of his fifteen-strong group for 'Mellow Madness' that he surprised everyone by deciding to go on tour with it. 'I have the feeling of this band,' he said. 'We have all the ages, and players from different schools who can play the entire spectrum of music. The young cats like George and Louis Johnson ('Boot' and 'Hen') on guitar and bass are only nineteen and twenty years old, but on the other side there's Frank Rosolino and Sahib Shihab on trombone and saxophone whose musical past dates back to Stan Kenton and Dizzy Gillespie. The fusion of these different schools makes it exciting to go into the studio or get up on the bandstand. I love it.'

They played seven major concerts in the United States and then toured twenty-four cities in Japan. 'It's really a strange feeling for me to be back on the road,' was Quincy's comment, 'having been locked up in a basement for over seven years with my film and TV work — or ill. But I really dig it. I don't think there is a better feeling for a musician than to see people in an audience moving and grooving to your music. The best part of it all is that I'm getting turned on from both sides: the band is burning behind me and the crowds are jumping in front. With a combination like that how could you help but be turned on?'

The balance of 1975 into 1976 was largely taken up by Quincy's determination to produce an A & M album with the Brothers Johnson, with his own next album collection 'I Heard That!!', and in working with New Yorker Tom Bahler on another Lesley Gore LP, 'Immortality'.

Full marks to him for spotting the enormous pop potential of George and Louis; but he then displayed an undoubted Midas Touch in recording them. Their album, 'Look Out for No. 1' upon release raced to No. 1 in the charts, earned another gold disc for over one million sales (in less than three months) and Quincy was named 'Record Producer of the Year'. As *Record World* put it, 'In the twenty-year period that Quincy Jones has been involved in the recording industry, he estimates that he has been a part of well over a thousand recordings. The astounding feature of it all is not the quantity of music he has created, but the quality and standard of excellence he's managed to achieve in every area he's pursued.'

Three further Johnson LPs have been released, all tremendous successes. 'George and Louis are extremely talented and creative young cats,' Quincy stresses. Of the follow-up to 'Look Out For No. 1' for instance, he says: 'After we finished our 28-city tour that summer (1976) we sat down in my studio and went through a battery of over fifty of their new tunes, picking and choosing ones we felt would work best for their album. I like to work with them in a manner of having a reasonable idea as to what we are going to cut once we get into the studio, as well as having a few holes open for songs that develop once we're working. On the first album we overcut, which I find to be the most effective way of recording, for once you are finished you can stand back from the record and see which tunes you want to use. This is the basic procedure I follow. . .'

The tour of 1976 was climaxed in the middle of September with four shows at New York's Madison Square Garden's Felt Farm, again all sell-outs. Billed as 'The Musical World Of Quincy Jones', it starred Quince, The Brothers Johnson, Q's newly-formed vocal group The Wattsline and a twenty-piece youth orchestra. And it propelled 'Renaissance Man' in yet another direction, that of the latest staging methods, the whole gamut from lazer-beam lighting to screen projection to coloured clouds.

'It's funny,' he recalls, 'because I've always referred to the direction I'm pursuing as an incestuous musical family, where all the elements . . . are constantly providing each other with new musical inspiration and influences. With that in mind, when I was mulling over my ideas for the concept of the show, I found that it would be dreadful to go out there and work within the traditional format of 'so and so' opening the show, the changeover, and then I would close. Consequently, when the curtains opened the entire cast was on the stage, the orchestra, dancers, the Brothers Johnson, Wattsline and myself. It made for a far more exciting show for me as the conductor, and hopefully — ultimately — the audience who had paid to see it. The real turn on came from the element of surprise, for the audience never knew exactly what was going to happen next. One minute we would do a full orchestral piece, the next it was a Brothers Johnson song, or a ballet to a pre-recorded medley of my film scores. It was a gas!'

Also in 1976 Quincy managed to squeeze in another session with Billy Eckstine. Together with A & M President Herb Alpert he arranged, conducted and produced a single, *The Best Thing*. 'Working with B again was marvellous. We've been friends for well over twenty-five years.' The reaction was so good that it extended itself into an album concept.

But his own major recording project of that year was to be 'I Heard That!!'.

'I Heard That!!' is a two-LP set. The second half consists of Q's award-winning items, ranging from *Summer In The City* to *Gula Matari* (in

Swaheli 'The Breaker of Rocks') to *Walking In Space*. But the first LP is all new music. The Brothers Johnson are represented again, together with a host of veterans (for the band is large again): Ernie Royal, Cat Anderson, Buddy Childers, Freddie Hubbard, Joe Newman, Marvin Stamm and Snooky Young in the trumpets — plus a few 'metal shaking' notes by Quincy himself. Meanwhile Dave Grusin uses Moog Polymoog Synthesizer, Minimoog, Moog Modular, ARP 2600, ARP Soloist, ARP String Ensemble, Oberheim 8-Voice, Oberheim Expander — and acoustic piano. All the electrified keyboards were programmed by Mike Boddicker. Quincy joined in occasionally on Fender Rhodes piano.

Just as important to this new material is the launching on record of QJ's permanent vocal group, The Wattsline, consisting of Mortonette Jenkins, Charles May, Sherwood Sledge, David Pridgen and Rodney Armstrong.

The composer/arranger had complained several times of the difficulty in recruiting his favourite singers at the exact moment he wanted them. As a result, he decided to audition for a group of his own, and to turn it into a national contest.

'It was kind of weird,' Quincy remembers. 'I got the idea of doing a contest because they really had no name. The group was put together out of necessity when I couldn't retain Valerie Simpson or Minnie Riperton for the road part. I auditioned well over a thousand singers in the quest to bring a permanent group together. I went through tapes, records and of course auditions. Once I had the people I wanted I was still stumped to come up with a name. So we sent out a press release about the contest thinking we would get a fair response and come up with a name. Well, that fair response came in the form of 50,000 letters and postcards, which led my office staff into a veritable state of hysterical misery. Ultimately a cat named James Washington, Jr from Detroit, came up with the name Wattsline, for the members were from Watts; and he felt they would have long-distance appeal. I dug the name right away.'

One of the Wattsline members, Charles May, contributed two musical items to 'I Heard That!!' as well as combining on two more with Q.

'Once again,' the latter says, 'I must refer to the incestuous musical family concept. Not only is Charles a damn' good singer, but he is a young guy who can play the piano, arrange, and write strong material. When he auditioned for the group he presented me with a tape of his tunes, and they really turned me on so I decided to use them. I'd be crazy to sit here and artistically stroke myself by saying that only I can write the material for a Quincy Jones album. My rule is, and will continue to be, as leader, producer and arranger of my own albums: if someone brings me a tune that

I dig, I like to take it and mould it into my own frame of reference.'

The title-number he co-wrote with Dave Grusin; and it immediately sets the mood of the album as being a consciously groovy one. Charles May's two songs follow this. *Things Could Be Worse For Me* features strong Dave Grusin plus the author's own deeply-felt soul singing. His lovely ballad *What Good Is A Song* then results in one of Quincy's finest arrangements for voices and ends with Tom Scott taking a lyricon solo. Side One closes with *You Have To Do It Yourself*, the disco-dance theme which Q had written for the children's TV show *Rebop*.

The flip-side opens with *There's A Train Leavin'*, a gospel-impregnated composition by Quincy with Charles May. The Wattsline are used as an intrumental colouring in places. Billy Preston (acoustic piano) and the Brothers Johnson are prominently featured, with trumpeter Snooky Young's plunger fill-ins towards the end reminding us of an earlier jazz era. *Midnight Soul Patrol* which follows highlights the guitar-playing of Louis Johnson, backed by Stanley Clarke and Alphonse 'Slim' Johnson on basses, the inventive Billy Cobham on drums and Moog drum and Dave Grusin and George Duke, keyboards. An added bonus is the flute solo by Quincy's longtime associate, Jerome Richardson, who also played lead to the saxes.

Ray Brown's *Brown Soft Shoe* has its composer and most distinguished bass-player locking in below what is largely a harmonica solo by Toots Thielmans, plus more Grusin, and Harvey Mason on drums. Then to complete the proceedings Stevie Wonder came into the studios carrying his own harmonica, the parts for his song *Superstition* and every intention of getting in on the action. The personnel for this last track reads like another musical 'Who's Who' of Jonesiana: the Brothers Johnson, The Wattsline, Stairsteps (by courtesy of Dark Horse Records), Billy Preston, Bill Withers added to the singers, Dave Grusin, David T Walker as an extra guitar, Stanley Clarke, bass, and not least the composer himself, wailing away in fine form. The sax solo is by Phil Woods, and it is Cat Anderson who takes his trumpet right up into outer space over the end.

With no further upsets to his health, for the remainder of the 1970s Quincy was kept as busy as ever. The key events were: the release of his 'Sounds . . . And Stuff Like That' LP; the work he did for Alex Haley's *Roots;* expanding Quincy Jones Productions to include both artists management and the formation of his own label; and his final superb album for A & M, 'The Dude' (released in 1981); plus, of course, his first auspicious involvement with Michael Jackson.

'Sounds . . . And Stuff Like That' was largely recorded on the West Coast, but for reasons of staggered availability some of the overdubbing took place in New York. The whole LP was then mixed by Quincy's favourite engineer, Bruce Swedien, back at Westlake Audio Inc, Los Angeles. Its music again concentrates heavily on soul singing and a very groovy rhythm section, fully electrified. But there is still a big brass contingent — and jazz solos pop up in the most unexpected places, by George Young, Tom Scott, Michael Brecker, Hubert Laws, Harry Lookovsky and Herbie Hancock, with the latter in addition contributing one of the songs, *Tell Me A Bedtime Story*. Otherwise the bulk of the composing was done by Quincy himself with Tom Behler, Stevie Wonder (*Superwoman, Where Were You When I Needed You*) and Lesley Gore (*Love Me By Name*). Quincy had Johnny Mandel in to help with some of the arranging.

Overall it is the quality of singing I find the most impressive feature of this particular collection, with the group vocals the best I've heard on any Quincy Jones LP. Admittedly with numbers like *I'm Gonna Miss You In The Morning* and *Love, I Never Had It So Good* (and the ones already listed) the singers had marvellous material to seize upon; but the solos from Valerie Simpson, Chaka Kahn, Charles May and Luther Vandross are all richly deserving of praise, as are those by Patti Austin, whom we encounter in Quincy's musical programming for the first time. In fact Quincy had borrowed her from Creed Taylor's CTI label for the sessions, and was so appreciative of her latest vocal abilities that he bided his time and then signed her to his own recording company.

Interestingly, a portion of the sleeve-notes for 'Sounds . . . And Stuff Like That' was contributed by Alex Haley, to whom Quincy mentioned that he had actually known Patti since she was three. 'Dinah Washington . . . brought her along to a session one day when I was recording the song *Blue Gardenia*. Dinah toyed with the song for eleven takes and Patti sang back every take with every single nuance. Three years old . . . I couldn't believe it!' Haley goes on to emphasize 'the well-spring of music which has poured from QJ . . . such an awesome array of talent as composer, arranger, conductor, producer, touring co-performer or some combination of all these with virtually a roll call among the greatest popular performers of our time.' This now leads us on to Quincy Jones's involvement with *Roots*.

Controversy still surrounds Alex Haley's book and the subsequent twelve-part TV serial. Haley, a former US Coast Guard and author of *The Autobiography Of Malcolm X*, has been accused of plagiarism, and even outright invention, during his many-year quest to uncover his cultural and family heritage in black Africa. Nor is his reputation and that of his TV colleagues unanimously high in The Gambia itself, where the story eventually took them. When in 1984, my own work took me briefly to the former French Senegal, I decided to cross into the nearby Gambian territories and, if possible, travel upriver in the wake of Mungo Park, the eighteenth-century Scottish explorer who took this route in his search of the sources of The Niger. Around Banjul (the former English Bathurst) I heard much talk of *Roots*, both of the book and the filming, especially in the vicinity of the Atlantic Hotel. Outside the tiny capital, though, they were hardly mentioned. I visited the notorious James Island and its ruined fortress where the slaves were penned under the most appalling conditions as they awaited transportation. Then I went on to Juffure, the village on the north bank of the river where Kunta Kinte, Haley's ancestor, was born. It is one of the poorest places in The Gambia. When I photographed the aged, infirm lady who had pieced together as a korah player and singer much of the history relative to Kunta Kinte's birth and taking by the slavers, she showed effusive gratitude over the few *dalasi* I left beside her.

In contrast, the success of *Roots* in the West has been almost beyond belief. Moreover, setting aside the controversies, it offers a very well-written text and has clearly been filmed with sensitivity. When Doubleday published the book it sold over 2,000,000 copies in hardback alone and in three weeks was America's No. 1 best-seller. In the meantime David Wolper and a TV syndicate had bought the film rights ahead of publication because of what they termed 'the social relevance that the book would have eventually on the world's consciousness'. They also filmed it with great visual beauty, and with excellent performances by Cicely Tyson, Len Gossett, Lorne Greene, Ed Asner, O.J. Simpson, Ben Vereen, Lloyd Bridges and the discovery of a nineteen-year-old drama student from USC, LaVar Burton, to play the leading role of Kunta Kinte.

Quincy was an obvious choice to do the music. Apart from previously knowing Haley as a friend, he had spent more than a decade studying the roots and transplants of Afro-American music. His subsequent score took the whole development through from jungle drums and korah string-singing to spirituals and gospel songs of America's black slums in the 1880s. Featured artists included Letta Mbulu, Caiphus Semenya, the James Cleveland Community Choir and percussionist Bill Summers. Reviews referred to his contribution as 'a vital part of one of the most important pieces of television in the history of the medium'.

Afterwards Alex Haley talked about the potentialities of a further collaboration with Quincy — which in turn sounded like the latter's longstanding 'dream' project, 'Evolution'. There was reference again to the eighty-minute two-LP set with gospel choir, symphony orchestra, big- and small-jazz groups, and dance. Also the thirteen public TV specials documenting the educational aspects of the project. To this was now added the idea of a book in thesis-form by Quincy and Haley covering the historical and educational elements of the research, following which there would be a travelling road show to present the music, and lastly a film with Haley doing the screenplay and Quincy directing. So far though this particular project has not yet taken wing, except insofar as Quincy has laid plans in his book-lined workroom/studio.

But it doesn't lessen Quincy's determination in intermingling (eventually) entertainment with education. 'The project *must* be educational,' he vows, 'because it is based on a great deal of historical research, and it must also be entertaining in order to reach a wide range of people. The public TV-show and a book to go with it will be primarily educational, with the entertainment element secondary, while the album, film and tour will be primarily entertainment and educational secondarily. The project is my masterwork in a sense, for I've spent so many years writing it. It's funny because I've had the utmost intentions of completing it for the past couple of years but, like cell divisions, it keeps growing and growing. I find myself discovering more and more information in writing more and more music. The job of editing will be intense.'

Meanwhile Quincy Jones Productions had been developing steadily under Q's chosen tillerman, Edward 'Ed' Eckstine — leaving Quincy more freedom to concentrate on the necessary musical decisions. Other executives included Melanie Ross, Pam Crocetti, Roger Jacobs and David Grayson. By the end of the 1970s they had formed their own label, Qwest Records Inc, and signed a world-wide distribution deal with the giant WEA group. Patti Austin was signed up and, by the early 1980s, Quincy had lured the gifted composer/singer James Ingram away from Wheel Records. He then won Frank Sinatra over to Qwest. But these events belong to the final chapter. . .

Engineer Bruce Swedien, 'Svensk', is almost a QJ staffer these days; and apart from their joint gastronomic interests — 'We often speak of the music on sessions in terms of *cooking* or *putting the spices together*' — has evolved what he calls the 'Acousonic Recording Process' to aid Quincy as a producer.

'Basically,' he says, 'the system uses either mag-link time-code or SMPTE time-code to synchronise multiple 24-track master tape recorders together, thereby greatly increasing the number of tracks available to use for the initial recording. Initially, my intention was to free Quince from the concern of not having enough tracks in the first multi-track recording to accomplish his rich, intricate musical ideas. I soon discovered that the system allowed me to record much more real stereophonic information by using pairs of tracks instead of the standard simple tracks so common in recording today. Many attempts have been made recently to achieve a more 'stereo' sound but these have been add-on gimmicks and really give no additional stereophonic dimension to the recording. They do, in fact, add distortion and other problems. The ARP adds no distortion as noise and, in fact, adds nothing but real stereo and its natural acoustical environment to the recording.'

Quincy still had one more album to make under his contract with A & M, and because his personal relations with the staff there have remained good, as usual he brought all his professional ambition to bear upon its completion. Starting off with *Ai No Corrida*, 'The Dude' is pure pop music, the companionship of Herbie Hancock and others notwithstanding. But for any listeners liking, say, Tamla Motown or other soul music there is very little room for disappointment. The potency of the beat is never lacking, Patti Austin and James Ingram blow up a storm with their singing, and in Rod Temperton Quincy has discovered another songwriter of Jim Webb-like abilities.

He himself announced 'total' satisfaction' with the LP, which in turn he dedicated to: 'My wife Peggy, my children Jolie, Tina, Quincy III, Kidada and Rashida, plus my grandchildren Donovan and Sonny, to my favourite singer and the daughter I don't recall asking for, Patti Austin, 'Happy Bread And Butter Pudding', and finally to his friend/brother over twenty-five years, Clarence Avant.

At this point he does not mention that, singing in with the backing group to James Ingram on *The Dude* track, there is a musical time-bomb called Michael Jackson. . .

Chapter 11

OFF GRAFFITTI, THE BRIGHT NEWCOMERS, OF GHOSTIES AND GHOULIES – AND OL' BLUE EYES IS BACK, AGAIN

The Michael Jackson story is an all-American dream as well as a show-business phenomenon. Normally, the artistic mortality rate among child superstars stands at well over ninety-five per cent. Freddie Bartholomew's later life was one of neglect, and drink. Shirley Temple (Black) failed to make it in adult films and became an ambassadress. The late Jackie Coogan and the living Dean Stockwell both had to work extraordinarily hard to become respected adult actors — in character parts. But now, and against all the current pop music trends, Michael Jackson has grown up to become the biggest superstar of our present decade. Even whether we will see his like again still seems debatable.

Michael first emerged as a public entertainer as the cheeky-faced eleven-year-old lead singer with The Jackson Five, a Tamla Motown group which also included his brothers Tito, Jermaine, Marlon, Jackie and later, Randy. They hailed from Gary, Indiana, the heavy industry city near Chicago and were managed by their father, Joe Jackson. At that time Michael's favourite artists were James Brown (of whom he could do a remarkably good impersonation), Aretha Franklin, Ray Charles and Chuck Berry. Joe Jackson soon realised the musical potential in his sons. He quit his factory job and got down to the task of rehearsing them properly. Often there were family rows because money intended for food and new clothes was invested instead in new instruments. But their father had it his own way and soon the boys would be rehearsing their music and a stage act for up to seven hours a day.

The lucky break came when Gladys Knight introduced the group to Tamla Motown — and her recommendation was to become the label's passport into a whole new generation of fans. With skilled choreography and saturation promotion the boys were soon topping the charts. The white community tried to exploit their teenage success by promoting The

Osmonds, another family quintet from Utah. But by this time The Jackson Five were too well established. The Osmonds had their blaze of glory, likewise David Cassidy, but where are they today?

With over 100 million records sold, and being a firm favourite on peak TV by the age of fourteen, Michael was already a dollar millionaire. Today his personal fortune is estimated at around $50 million and growing at the rate of $10 million more per year.

However: Michael was growing up fast and clearly changes had to be made. In October 1971 Motown released *Got To Be There* as his first solo record. It was the start of a regular flow of singles and albums — and a further big success in the charts. In 1975 he switched labels to Epic, the division of CBS, and the adulation plus hysteria which now surrounds his every new record or personal appearance, or even press release, began to grow into a whole new added dimension. In the 1980s he is quite simply the hottest property in the whole of American show-business, and probably throughout the world. As Quincy Jones himself comments: 'The 1950s were Elvis Presley's decade, in the '60s we had The Beatles, the '70s belonged to 'Star Wars', and now the '80s are definitely Michael's'.

Michael Jackson is still only in his twenties, with dazzling good looks and a natural, abundantly skilled performer whether singing, acting or dancing. He is also priceless, a star whose appeal defies almost every rule. When approached to perform at a huge US festival in California in 1983, the organisers quoted him a fee of $1½ million. 'You're not even close,' his agents replied. . .'

Quincy Jones remembers being impressed by the poise Michael showed when, aged twelve, he sang *Ben* at the Academy Awards ceremony. Later he met him during a party at the home of Sammy Davis, Jr. But the two did not really come together professionally until filming started of *The Wiz* (Sydney Lumet's black version of *The Wizard Of Oz* starring Diana Ross). QJ had been appointed musical supervisor for the project, with Michael hired to play the Scarecrow.

'In *The Wiz*,' Quincy says, 'I heard more in Michael Jackson than the little, high voice I'd last heard with The Jackson Five. In the studio I found him to be a very disciplined worker — a legacy of early Motown training — with none of the ego problems one might predict from a young man who had been the subject of wild adulation from the age of eleven. Michael's a truth machine. He's got the balance between the wisdom of a sixty-year-old and the enthusiasm of a child.' Since then Quincy at times calls him 'Smelly', because of Michael's highly attuned nose for good business and the right musical decisions.

In making *The Wiz* they became firm friends and, even more significantly, solid working partners. Quincy figured that if the keys in which Michael had been singing were dropped, even by as little as a semitone, he would uncover a more flexible range of expression and so be able to tackle adult love songs with greater conviction. In turn Michael suggested that Quincy might become the producer of certain of his solo records at Epic. This was how the monumental commercial successes of both 'Off The Wall' and 'Thriller' had their beginnings. (To date 'Thriller' alone has sold more than 30,000,000 albums, and Quincy refers to Michael Jackson as 'The Citizen Kane of the videos'!)

Even when they are not involved on the same project Quincy is still the respected authority Michael turns to for musical and human guidance. Riches have forced him into a Howard Hughes-type existence, hidden away and guarded twenty-four hours a day in his Californian Tudor-style mansion. He cannot go out shopping without being mobbed. So he relies on visits from his inner circle of friends, his stack of video-tapes and his mini zoo, the stars of which are a South American llama ('Louise'), a couple of deer ('Prince & Princess'), a sheep he calls 'Mister Tibbs' and, not least, a boa constrictor aptly-named 'Muscles'. But scarcely an evening passes when he doesn't call Quincy Jones 'just to talk things over. . .'

'Off The Wall' was released in 1979 and features songs by Jackson himself (*Don't Stop 'Til You Get Home, Working Day And Night, Get On Floor*), Rod Temperton (*Rock With You, Off The Wall, Burn This Disco Out*), Paul McCartney (*Girlfriend*), Tom Bahler (*She's Out Of My Life*) and Carol Bayer Sager (*It's The Falling In Love*).

Quincy did very little of the arranging himself, preferring to mastermind everything from the control-room: the strings and brass and accompanying singers, the forceful rhythm, helping Bruce Swedien with remixing and, not least, directing and encouraging Michael. With the latter he insisted on 'live' performances in the studio, for freshness of expression and also to gain the maximum impetus from the busy, intricate patterns of the rhythm section. No overdubs, he said; and it worked. As one writer/listener (Geoff Brown) put it: 'The fast dance tracks finally unveil Michael's armoury of expressive vocal mannerisms. He unleashes a battery of gasps, grunts, booms, bomps, squeaks, squeals, whoops, laughs, chuckles, 'chucks' and clucks. In fact, any noise the larynx can make that can be used in a rhythmic way. While on Rod Temperton's mid-tempo songs he's given a smooth and easy back-up for the breathier, less casual treatments.' McCartney's *Girlfriend* and Tom Bahler's *She's Out Of My Life* are more clearly standard ballads, the former fairly cheekily (and rhythmically) done, the latter heavily laden with strings and mournful guitars. Bahler's song was also a first 'take' although others were attempted. Michael had a few doubts, but Quincy persuaded him which take was best.

Four singles from the LP, *Don't Stop 'Til You Get Enough*, *Off The Wall*, *Rock With You* and *She's Out Of My Life* each made the No. 1 slot in the US charts. A fifth, *Girlfriend*, no doubt helped by its McCartney origins, made the British charts and is reputed to have sold seven million copies world-wide.

Having been acclaimed and suitably rewarded for 'Off The Wall', and before the advent of 'Thriller', Quincy returned to his own offices and the job of turning his belief in Patti Austin's talents into a further success story. He had not only known her from the age of three, she had toured with his ill-fated *Free And Easy* show at the age of nine, and had become his favourite session singer — as well as appearing on albums with Paul Simon ('Still Crazy After All These Years'), Billy Joel ('Just The Way You Are') and Frankie Valli ('Our Day Will Come'). Quincy now produced a first album of her own for Qwest — 'Every Home Should Have One' — which in turn led to a hit single *Baby Come To Me*, a duet by Patti with Quincy's other new signing, James Ingram.

A tremendously versatile singer, since then and for her second LP simply entitled 'Patti Austin', Quincy has introduced a whole bank of new writers and generally let each co-produce his own material — Clif Magness, Glen Ballard, Narada Michael Walden, David Pack, Jeffrey Cohen, Ollie E Brown and Preston Glass. He himself produced only the opening track, *It's Gonna Be Special*, taken up from the John Travolta/Olivia Newton-John film *Two Of A Kind*. *Rhythm Of The Street* (Narada Michael Walden) in a remixed version was the selected title for a single issue and again did well.

Clearly a different approach was required for James Ingram's solo album. Ingram, from Akron, Ohio, was very much his own man, a songwriter, synthesizer- and keyboards-player, and no mean arranger. He had picked up a Grammy award as 'Best R & B Artist' for his contributions to Quincy's 'The Dude', had worked with Ray Charles and since then shared the hit single with Patti Austin. So for his first solo album on Qwest, 'It's Your Night' Quincy just let him do his own thing and kept a very gentle hand on the tiller as overall producer. The single released from the LP, *She Loves Me (The Best That I Can Be)*, backed by *It's Your Night* is at the time of writing the most frequently broadcast of the Qwest new pop releases.

The completion of 'Thriller' was not so easily achieved. Michael Jackson, more a recluse than ever with his animals and piles of movies (he's reportedly watched *E.T.* over fifty times and cried each time), has followed his mother Katherine into her embracing of religion as a Jehovah's Witness. He has not used the discipline of this to push his fame and shout about it. He reads the Bible each day, attends Kingdom Hall three times a week, is into neither drugs nor drink and believes his talent comes from God. Even so, he is also aware of his talent's value in the market-place. He considers that he has been put on earth to entertain, to please his audiences, to bring joy and enrichment. The fact he says he never really knew how, or why, he was able to sing and dance from an early age emphasises his notion that the gift is divine providence.

At the same time he is a perfectionist and expects high standards in management as well as from musicians. Although close to his parents, as a businessman his attitude remains wholly pragmatic about management decisions. He refuses to allow even family ties to get in the way of making the best business deal possible. For instance, in March 1983 two important management contracts expired — one with his father Joe, the other with Ron Weisner and Freddy De Mann's firm. So far, Michael has not renewed either contract, although Weisner and De Mann were left to work on certain contracts, including 'Thriller' and a follow-up LP for Epic. Meanwhile Joe Jackson, in an extraordinary outburst to *Billboard* magazine in June 1983, announced that the Weisner/De Mann contract would *never* be renewed. 'There are a lot of teachers,' he shouted angrily. 'A lot of people are whispering in Michael's ear. But we know who they are. They're only in it for the money. I was there before it started and I'll be there after it ends.' He added that he had only signed with Weisner/Mann in the first place because he needed 'white help in dealing with the corporate structure at CBS'. Michael disowned these last words as an overt accusation of racial prejudice.

Against the background of these various arguments, an even bigger row occurred when MCA tried to put out a storybook album of Steven Spielberg's *E.T.* with Michael featured as the narrator, and Quincy Jones as artistic consultant. CBS sought $2 million damages from MCA, plus an injunction stopping their marketing a record because it would interfere with the sales of Michael's own new LP.

So much for the circumstances under which 'Thriller' would be made — although in the end it was built up to become a triumph. Michael opted for the same team who had served so well in making 'Off The Wall': producer Quincy Jones, songwriter Rod Temperton, plus certain key rhythm players (Greg Phillinganes, David Williams, Michael Boddicker) and arranger

Jerry Hey's brass section. Quincy worked mainly on the vocal groups and rhythm section parts — as well as alongside Bruce Swedien in the box.

Michael decided, in conjunction with Quincy, to include three Rod Temperton numbers, two love songs, *Baby Be Mine* and *The Lady In My Life*, together with the title track (for which the jokey/horror film voice of veteran Hollywood actor Vincent Price was also, inspiredly, recruited). They then chose *Human Nature*, a delightful ballad by Jeff Porcaro and John Bettis, and PYT (*Pretty Young Thing*) which Quincy had co-authored with James Ingram. The singer himself contributed four items: *Wanna Be Startin' Somethin'*, *Beat It*, *Billie Jean* and *finally*, *The Girl Is Mine*, which he intended to do as a duet with his friend Paul McCartney.

Within another immensely varied collection, oddly it is the songs by the other contributors which tend to be light and happy-sounding, or alternatively spookily novel like *Thriller*, while Michael's own have moodiness and even a degree of anger, a *volte-face* after the creamier graffitti he had written in his early career. It is as if he needs to escape the forced seclusion and fantasies of his present life for a different kind of reality in music. In *Wanna Be Startin' Somethin'*, to begin with he hits out at gossip columnists, especially those who link his every action with a possible marriage, an unwanted pregnancy or a nervous breakdown. Further on in the song he lambasts two-faced friends, and of Billie Jean complains that her false charms are so regulated that 'they called her mouth a motor'. In *Beat It* he emphasises the need for self-preservation even if the media have turned you into a prisoner. 'You have to show them that you're not really scared,' he sings. While in the *Billie Jean* song itself he returns to the subject of an attractive woman who accuses the singer of fathering her child.

As his own biographer Geoff Brown states the case: 'This is pure autobiography. Like many pop stars Michael has been the object of accusations and paternity suits, but one could not easily imagine a less likely candidate for such a guilty secret. "Billy Jean is not my lover," he repeats to make sure we get the message. The song even encouraged one Lydia Murdock to record an 'answer' to it with *Superstar*, which puts Billie Jean's side of this imaginary story.'

Brown adds: 'From the celebration and partying spirit on 'Off The Wall' Michael has laid open his real inner feelings on 'Thriller' to reveal a much darker side. He shows himself as a young man on the defensive, but with a nucleus of unbreakable resolves, determined to have the last word because he's convinced truth is on his side. These tracks ensure that as well as a series of technically accomplished, glossy, danceable pop hits, we're also given an insight into the serious concerns of a more adult Michael. In the end, 'Thriller' is about the fight between duplicity and honesty.'

Even now though the album would not reach its huge potential market before there was a final hiccup. Q had been working on a Donna Summers LP which took longer than expected. This left him three months to make and meet the CBS release-date for 'Thriller'. Three months then cut into by parallel work on the *'ET Storybook'* for Steven Spielberg. 'It almost killed us, but we made it,' Quincy later told *Down Beat*. 'I had two studios going. We just rocked around the clock until we finished.

'Then we had a scary thing happen. We finished *ET*, and Michael's record was down to mix and master. But then the test-presing of 'Thriller' arrived: to be passed for release.' And they were horrified! Michael cried. 'It sounded like shit, man. We knew it wouldn't hold. It was *terrible*.' The sides were too long; which had reduced the sound level. Also, 'Basically the mixes were sloppy because we were hurrying. Overall, there were a lot of bad judgements from being hasty and tired. Adrenalin turns your ears into something else. So we decided to hell with the deadline, 'cause they were really on our backs. So we took time off . . . took one tune a day and brought this baby home. And that's what we did. If the record had gone out, it would never have been *over*, it would have been a disaster. I'll never forget that day.'

Michael Jackson faced further fights when his 1984 so-billed 'Victory' tour of the US blasted off in Kansas City. This time no less than $100 million in guarantees were being quoted, and according to the sober reporters of *Newsweek* the dust is more likely to be settled before the various lawsuits connected with 'Jackson Fever'.

Sometimes success can be so colossal, however, that not even a Pied Piper's voiced frustrations can interfere with its progress. As regards 'Thriller', it not only dwarfed 'Off The Wall' in sales; it achieved that in a much shorter space of time. By June of 1983 *The Girl Is Mine, Billie Jean, Beat It* and *Wanna Be Startin' Somethin'* had all topped the US charts and outsold with ease the previous LP's crop. 'Thriller' dominated the LP charts in the US and Britain — and when *Billie Jean* became the top single in the American and British pop charts, Michael also became the first artist to top the American R & B, and pop LP, and singles charts, all at the same time. In Canada, with a much smaller population than the US, nevertheless 'Thriller' became a gold, platinum, double, triple, quadruple, and quin-tuple platinum disc. *Billie Jean* the single went to gold, platinum and double platinum; but *Beat It* only managed gold and platinum!

By August CBS was able (justly) to call Michael Jackson 'The Number One Artist In The World' . . . and they presented him with 36 different awards from 19 different countries.

Then the video clips started selling and a whole new marketing bonanza was under way. The main 'Thriller' segment, shot by John Landis of 'An American Werewolf In London' fame, at an estimated cost of $4.5 million for just thirteen minutes of fare, has proved immensely popular almost everywhere. No doubt even in Transylvania!

Quincy Jones's other major *coup* so far of the 1980s took place on 13, 16 and 17 April, 1984 at A & R Recording Studios in New York City, and again on 17 May at Ocean Way Recording Studios in Los Angeles. On those days Francis Albert Sinatra made an album under the auspices of Quincy Jones for the latter's Qwest label. It was then released to coincide with the 1984 Los Angeles Olympic Games and is called 'L.A. Is My Lady'.

The title-song lyric was written by Alan and Marilyn Bergman, and the music by Quincy Jones and his wife Peggy. Otherwise the contents of the LP are earlier, quality standards: *The Best Of Everything* (by Fred Ebb), *How Do You Keep The Music Playing* (again by the Bergmans with Michel Legrand), *Teach Me Tonight* (Sammy Cahn and Gene De Paul), *It's All Right With Me* (Cole Porter), *Mack The Knife* (by Brecht and Kurt Weill and with an English lyric by Marc Blitzstein, cleverly changed in places for this LP), *Until The Real Thing Comes Along* (another of Sammy Cahn's songs), Harold Arlen's *Stormy Weather*, *If I Should Lose You* (by Robin and Rainger), *A Hundred Years From Today* by Young and Washington, and finally *After You've Gone* by Cremer and Layton.

The bands which Quincy Jones assembled were again as good as any that could be heard in the whole of the United States, from Jon Faddis, Dizzy Gillespie's protégé on lead-trumpet, to Quincy's favourite multi-reedman Jerome Richardson, and the ex-Basie saxists, Frank Foster and Frank Wess, and on to other celebrated players who simply wanted to be on the LP because it was with Sinatra — Lionel Hampton (vibes), Michael Brecker (saxes), Ray Brown (bass) and Steve Gadd (drums). Also there was George Benson on guitar, always the sharpest dresser on the sessions and who insisted his headphones be so adjusted that they wouldn't upset his hairstyle! Major Holley (bass) was brought in for one of the sessions because Quincy wanted to feature his additional celebrated 'grunted' vocalese to accompany *Mack The Knife*.

The great singer, who revels in 'comebacks', could not resist either these songs or these musicians. But everything had to be 100% because he hates second takes after he has his own performance together and ready. So

Quincy had not left anything to chance. There was always a late afternoon rehearsal for the musicians, and with an informal buffet on hand — chicken wings, salad, shrimp and macaroons. The enthusiasm was infectious. Jon Faddis wondered whether he should not take the trumpet part on *Stormy Weather* up an octave. Quincy winced. There were forty musicians on the New York sessions, plus friends (invited) including Milt Jackson, Sylvia Syms, Michael Jackson, Michael Bennett, Roberta Flack, Jimmy Webb.

The band was rehearsed and waiting now. Once Frank arrived accompanied by his wife Barbara, the ritual began. He listened carefully to a run through of the first score, then removed his blue windcheater and said, 'All right, now let's make a record'. In all, they recorded eleven numbers (ten destined to be masters). A proposed twelfth title, *Body And Soul,* had been prepared but Frank rejected it; he had done the song before for Columbia and did not believe he could add anything new to it. Quincy, hating to see an arrangement go on the shelf, said with little hope, 'We have better microphones now.' Mister S. didn't change his mind.

Never a time-waster, in the course of the album he averaged 25 minutes per song.

But then — at 8.12 pm on 18 April precisely — on the seventh floor of the pizza-smelling building which houses A & R Studios, he called for drinks to be served. He then listened to everthing back, all three nights' work. The room was crowded with players and guests. They smiled at each other, filled with self-congratulation at being present for a Sinatra session and playback. However, as they drank and relished the occasion, so the two men who mattered most were listening attentively. At the end of the tapes there was a pause. Then, 'It sounds okay, Q' the singer told his conductor/producer. Take it all back to LA and mix it. I'm happy.

'Oh — and by the way, thanks a lot. . .'

Whether it places a baton in his hand as he faces a symphony orchestra or has him supervising the electric sounds of a pop unit, nothing in music seems to be beyond Quincy Jones. Yet there is a unifying thread in all of his activity which any portrait must attempt to isolate and follow. For Quincy Jones's music-making has a number of distinguishing features. Although continuously changing and developing it is also easily identifiable — *with him* — and it offers us inherent qualities: of excitement with good taste, and of consummate professionalism with a recognition of its ultimate audience. Just as importantly, everything in it stems from his private roots and growth. These are melodic and rhythmic, alternately sacred and

101

secular, but certainly consistent — and as such they have taken jazz, the blues and soul music into areas of public entertainment where no one had dared go with them before.

Worthwhile music in any form invariably has to battle for recognition and acceptance at the outset. Then, when the battle is won, it becomes part of our everyday lives. Here, in this book, therefore, I have endeavoured to trace, in a concentrated form, the course of one musician of great natural talent and curiosity who has aimed high, faced up to the problems, still believed in himself — *and won*. Quince, or Q, or, to use his full name, Quincy Delight Jones is unlike any other musical personality. That is one of the necessary qualities for being a master.

A CODA FOR QUINCY JONES

Often, when younger, driving down through France but taking the higher, hillier routes, I'd be surprised at the number of butterflies of all sizes and vivid colours just sitting on the road. Often too, unfortunately, I would roll over some of them. Until one day I remarked upon it to my great friend, Roger Lacroix of Nîmes and the Cévennes. 'Didn't you know?' he said. 'Like most of us they're carnivores. And there are always beetles and flies and other small creatures crushed by passing cars which they can fly to for food. 'But,' he added, 'they eat delicately and take only what they need. Not like the magpies or those terrible crows who in their greed will rip and tear at everything.' Which in turn reminded me of a boyhood in Cheshire where the crows peck the eyes out of living sheep trapped by the snows in winter.

Quincy: in a long and distinguished musical career you have used the services of many people, and helped a lot more; and I have never heard one harsh word uttered against you. My wishes for you in the future are that you remain as natural as the pattern made by the dust on a butterfly's wings. That the pattern is never marred or the wings damaged. I'd hate to think you couldn't fly any more because I know with you the love of flight has become effortless.

APPENDIX

Motion Pictures:
THE BOY IN THE TREE – Swedish: Arne Sucksdorff
THE PAWNBROKER – Independent: Rod Steiger
MIRAGE – Universal: Gregory Peck
THE SLENDER THREAD – Paramount: Sidney Poitier, Anne Bancroft
WALK, DON'T RUN – Columbia: Cary Grant, Samantha Eggar
THE DEADLY AFFAIR – Columbia: James Mason
ENTER LAUGHING – Columbia: José Ferrer
BANNED – Universal: Robert Wagner
IN THE HEAT OF THE NIGHT – Mirisch: Rod Steiger, Sidney Poitier
IN COLD BLOOD – Columbia: Robert Blake, Scott Wilson
JIGSAW – Universal: Harry Guardino, Hope Lange
A DANDY IN ASPIC – Columbia: Laurence Harvey, Mia Farrow
THE LOVE OF IVY – Palomar: Sidney Poitier
THE HELL WITH HEROES – Universal: Rod Taylor, Claudia Cardinale
THE SPLIT – MGM: Jim Brown, Gene Hackman, Ernest Borgnine
MAC KENNA'S GOLD – Columbia: Gregory Peck, Omar Sharif
THE ITALIAN JOB – Paramount: Michael Caine, Noel Coward
THE LOST MAN – Universal: Sidney Poitier
BOB AND CAROL AND TED AND ALICE – Columbia: Elliot Gould,
   Dyan Cannon
THE OUT OF TOWNERS – Paramount: Jack Lemmon, Sandy Dennis
THE LAST OF THE MOBILE HOTSHOTS – Warner Bros: James Coburn
JOHN AND MARY – 20th Century Fox: Dustin Hoffman, Mia Farrow
CACTUS FLOWER – Columbia: Ingrid Bergman, Walter Matthau
THEY CALL ME MISTER TIBBS – Mirisch: Sidney Poitier, Martin Landau
BROTHER JOHN – Columbia: Sidney Poitier
YAO OF THE JUNGLE – The Harold Robbins Company

SHELIA – Getty-Fromkess: Brenda Sykes
THE ANDERSON TAPES – Columbia: Sean Connery
$$ – Columbia: Warren Beatty, Goldie Hawn
THE HOT ROCK – 20th Century Fox: Robert Redford, George Segal
THE NEW CENTURIONS – Columbia: George C. Scott, Stacey Keach
THE GETAWAY – National General: Steve McQueen, Ali MacGraw

Animated Films:
EGGS – John and Faith Hubley
OF MEN AND DEMONS – John and Faith Hubley

Television:
THE WORLD OF ENTERTAINMENT ROASTS REDD FOXX – ABC
SANFORD AND SON – Redd Foxx – NBC
DUKE ELLINGTON . . . WE LOVE YOU MADLY! – CBS-Tandem Productions
THE BILL COSBY SHOW – NBC
THE NEW BILL COSBY SHOW – CBS
IRONSIDE – Raymond Burr – NBC
HEY! LANDLORD – Sandy Baron, Will Hutchins – NBC
DIG – John and Faith Hubley – CBS (animated ecology special)
REBOP-PBS (children's educational show)
ROOTS – ABC
CASSIDY AND TORRES – ABC – a series pilot

Awards and Nominations: Oscar
IN COLD BLOOD – Academy Awards nomination, Best Original
    Score – 1967
THE EYES OF LOVE – Best Song nomination – Lyric by Bob Russell – 1968
FOR LOVE OF IVY – Best Song nomination – Lyric by Bob Russell – 1969
MUSICAL CONDUCTOR AND ARRANGER – Academy Awards – 1971

Emmy:
THE BILL COSBY SHOW – Outstanding Achievement in Musical
    Composition
SOMETHING MORE (MORE THAN LOVE) – Best Original Song from a
    Motion Picture – 1971

Grammy Nominations, Awards:

I CAN'T STOP LOVING YOU – A & M single – National Academy of Recording Arts and Sciences – Best Instrumental Arrangement – 1963 Grammy Award

WALKING IN SPACE – A & M album – Best Jazz Performance by a Large Group – 1969 Grammy Award

SOUL FLOWER – A & M single – Best Contemporary Instrumental Performance – 1969 Grammy Nomination

GULA MATARI – A & M album – Best Instrumental Composition, Best Instrumental Arrangement – 1970 Grammy Nomination.

SMACKWATER JACK – A & M album – Best Instrumental Pop, Rock or Folk Performance – 1972 Grammy Award

SUMMER IN THE CITY – A & M single – Best Instrumental – 1973 Grammy Award . . . plus approximately thirty other various Gramy nominations

Other Awards:

DOWN BEAT – New Star Arranger – 1956

DOWN BEAT – Readers Poll – 1960

DOWN BEAT – Critics Poll – 1960, both for Best Arranger

DUTCH EDISON AWARD – Hip Hits – 1964

SECOND PLACE, BRAZIL INT'L SONG FESTIVAL – 'The World Goes on – 1967

ANTONIO CARLOS JOBIM AWARD – Best Arranger – Brazil Int'l Song Festival – 1967

DUTCH EDISON AWARD – Walking In Space – 1969

DOWN BEAT – Readers Poll – Best Arranger – 1970/71

BILLBOARD TRENDSETTERS AWARD – 1970/71

DOWN BEAT – Critics Poll – Best Arranger, Composer, Recording Artist – 1974

JOHNSON PUBLICATIONS AWARD – Best Arranger, Composer, Recording Artist – 1974

In addition, there is now a Quincy Jones scholarship given each year by the Berklee School of Music in Boston, Massachussetts.

AUTHOR'S ACKNOWLEDGEMENTS

Wherever possible I have credited writers, journals and other sources quoted from inside the text of the book. However, my thanks and gratitude go to a number of people in addition:

To my painstaking discographer, Tony Middleton; editors, David Burnett James and John Bright-Holmes; and publisher, Ian Morley-Clarke.

To the publicity and promotion staffs at A & M Records and WEA. Both have been extremely prompt and helpful with corroborative information, while the latter have sent me the discs by Patti Austin and James Ingram which previously I did not own.

The words used in Chapter 3 about Quincy with Lionel Hampton's band are mine, nevertheless I was fortunate in being able to double-check the facts alongside an article by my friend Alun Morgan which appeared in the April 1955 issue of *Jazz Monthly*.

Further, I had the chance to talk with Count Basie before his death about Quincy Jones, both with his band and in accompanying Frank Sinatra. I feel fairly certain, as a result, that I have proceeded along the right lines.

Extra affirmations have resulted from conversations with many more musicians, not least Richard Davis who first made the observation to me that Quincy Jones has a lot in common with the versatility of the artists of the Renaissance. . .

WE ARE THE WORLD . . .

Since completing the main text for publication, I have learned of the most important activity by Quincy in 1985 as producer of *We Are The World,* the special single designed to raise money in aid of the Ethiopian relief fund. Following the success of a disc by Band Aid in the British and US charts (£8,000,000 derived from initial sales), it was decided that an all-American single with an even larger collection of 'star' names might make even more for the stricken peoples of the Horn of Africa (estimated earnings from this record: $200,000,000). For *We Are The World* QJ did much of the recruiting as well as the production; and he said to each arriving celebrity: 'Leave your ego right there at the door.'

Some forty-five people took part. Prominent among them, Cyndi Lauper, Michael Jackson, Lionel Ritchie, Willie Nelson, Bruce Springsteen (playing guitar as well), Diana Ross, Stevie Wonder, Kenny Rogers, Kenny Loggins, Jeffrey Osborne, Lindsey Buckingham, Brenda Russell, Huey Lewis and The News, James Ingram, Smokey Robinson, Daryl Hall and John Oates, Paul Simon, Bob Geldof (of the British Band Aid record), Wayne Jennings, Bob Dylan, Sheila E, Ruth, Anita and June Pointer, Ray Charles, Dan Ackroyd, Dionne Warwick, Christopher Cross, Dara Bernard, Michael McDonald, Al Jarreau, Billy Joel, Marlon Jackson, Bette Midler and Harry Belafonte. The sessions took place in the Lion Share and A & M Studios, Los Angeles and the pressing and distribution went to CBS Records and its licencees. However: the actual release was then delayed in order that the British Band Aid single could complete its run in the US charts and so raise as many dollars as possible. Meanwhile, at a press presentation of *We Are The World* only the song's chorus was played, as a safeguard against piracy.

We Are The World itself, otherwise known as 'USA For Africa' is a joint compositon by Michael Jackson and Lionel Ritchie. . .

As regards his own future plans Quincy indicates his clear determination to produce a film based on Alice Walker's *The Colour Purple*. He has just finished a new solo album which features Sarah Vaughan and organist Jimmy Smith. But already in his Los Angeles business office, with its photographs of heroes and associates like Miles Davis and Count Basie, plus its bank of ten flashing phone-lines, there are note pads printed with *The Colour Purple* on them.

'There's a book that tore my heart out — it's so beautiful,' he told Zan Stewart of *Down Beat* magazine recently. 'Reading it has been one of the most incredible experiences I've had in my life. For fifteen years people have wanted me as executive producer of films, mainly to get the musical connection and just have me as a spectator. But I want to be in the physical process of making the film. That's what's nice. It's an unbelievable project, just loaded with rich music that dates from 1905 to 1940, so the music of Scott Joplin, Robert Johnson, Bessie Smith and Coleman Hawkins will be included. Imagine a film where part of the tapestry is a Hawk solo and one of the leads is just mumbling along with the solo. That turns me on.

'And it reminds me. There was an album, I think it was 'Hawk In Flight', which if you played it at 45 rpm instead of 33 rpm, you'd hear a version of *There Will Never Be Another You* that sounds just like Bird (Charlie Parker). Hearing that blew me away because you could see the roots and the connection. It opened up a big door for my head; the nuances were identical, all of them.'

So: his obsession with beginnings, and the transformation of earlier, especially African music into modern American music remains as potent as ever. Which, Zan Stewart suggested, the film is giving him another chance to work on.

'The evolution, yeah, exactly. It's amazing how things work out. You don't plan it. I started around 1970, just digging — really didn't know why except I was just interested in it — the evolution of our music. After being in the business twenty-five years, I felt it would be fun to go back and see the exact sources. Research. I thought it would take two or three months, but I got hung up, ultimately going back to 479 AD to the Moors, the Spanish Inquisition, then following thirty-four tribes from West Africa to Brazil up to the West Indies then on to New Orleans, Virginia and so forth. It just blew me away again. The whole idea of drums being banned in 1672 because the slave owners knew it was a communicative device. To ban the drums did something to the music. That was in the Protestant colonies. In the Catholic colonies they were *getting down* – the Spanish, French – with food, music, everything. That's where it all happened. A lot of people were oppressed and restricted by the Anglicans. But when it was time to get rhythmic again, everything had to be redefined rhythmically, so a hybrid music came out of it. The film plays a role in underscoring all this.'

Also he has projected a musical with Mike Nichols. Its working headline is 'Speak Easy': about the 1920s and '30s.

Zan Stewart: 'So here you are producing all this modern music like Michael Jackson, and then turn around and dig way back!'

'That's what's so great about it – the whole menu. Why not, man? I love the notion of what that's all about, the whole range. It's so real and so strong. I love the chance to go from a Michael Jackson situation to my own album to *The Colour Purple*, where we have a really valid reason for using the music of that period, other than simply wanting to expose it.'

PEOPLE GET ALL HUNG UP WITH THE EVOLUTION OF THIS MUSIC, SAYING 'YOU'RE NOT INTO JAZZ ANYMORE'. BULLSHIT. IT'S ALL THE SAME THING TO ME. (QJ, *Down Beat*, 1985)

SELECT DISCOGRAPHY

The discography covers records issued under Quincy Jones's name plus other sessions referred to in the text. Not included are singles, EPs, compilations, soundtracks and shows. The following abbreviations have been used: (arr) arrangement; (as) alto-sax; (b) bass; (bars) baritone sax; (cl) clarinet; (cond) conductor; (d) drums; (fl) flute; (flh) flugelhorn; (frh) French horn; (g) guitar; (tb) trombone; (tp) trumpet; (ts) tenor-sax; (vbs) vibraphone; (vcl) vocal. Only records issued in (Eu) Europe and (Am) United States of America are noted. Locations: LA (Los Angeles), NYC (New York City).

Tony Middleton.
London, March 1985

QUINCY JONES SWEDISH-AMERICAN ALL STARS
Art Farmer (tp); Jimmy Cleveland, Ake Persson (tb); Arne Domnerus (as, cl); Lars Gullin (bars); Bengt Hallberg (p); Simen Brehm (d); Alan Dawson (d); Quincy Jones (arr). *Stockholm, November 10, 1953*

POGO STICK	Metronome (Eu) EP30, Esquire (Eu) EP5
LIZA	" "
JONES' BONES	Metronome (Eu) EP31, Esquire (Eu) EP20
SOMETIMES I'M HAPPY	" "

All four titles on Metronome (Eu) MLP15020, Prestige (Am) LP172.

QUINCY JONES AND THE ALL STARS
Ernie Royal, Bernie Glow, Al Porcino, Jimmy Nottingham (tp); J.J. Johnson, Urbie Green, Jimmy Cleveland (tb); Herbie Mann (fl); Dave Schildkraut (as); Sonny Stitt, Al Cohn (ts); Jack Nimitz (bars); Horace Silver (p); Oscar Pettiford (b); Osie Johnson, Art Blakey (d); Quincy Jones (arr). *NYC, February 25, 1955*

GRASSHOPPER	Columbia (Am) CL1970, CS8770

CL1970 = CBS (Eu) BPG62141, S62141

QUINCY JONES AND HIS ORCHESTRA
Ernie Royal, Reunald Jones, Joe Newman, Jimmy Nottingham (tp); Sonny Russo, Urbie Green, Jimmy Cleveland (tb); Marshall Royal, Bobby Playter (as); Frank Wess, Sam Taylor (ts); Charlie Fowlkes (bars); Hank Jones (p); Milt Hinton (b); Osie Johnson (d); Quincy Jones (arr).   *NYC, December, 1955*
      FLYING HOME   Decca

including Billy Byers (tb); Al Cohn, Zoot Sims (ts); Hank Jones (p); Don Lamond (d); Quincy Jones (arr).   *NYC, 1956*
      LULLABY OF BIRDLAND   RCA-Victor (Am) EPA672, LPM1146

QUINCY JONES ALL STARS
Art Farmer (tp); Jimmy Cleveland (tb); Herbie Mann (fl, ts); Gene Quill (as); Lucky Thompson (ts)-1; Zoot Sims (ts)-2; Jack Nimitz (bars); Hank Jones (p); Charles Mingus (b); Charlie Persip (d); 'Brother Soul' Milt Jacksom (vbs); Father John Crowley (hand claps); Quincy Jones (arr). *NYC. September 14, 1956*
      SERMONETTE -1   ABC-PARAMOUNT (Am) ABC149
      EVENING IN PARIS -2   "

Art Farmer (tp); Jimmy Cleveland (tb); Herbie Mann (fl); Phil Woods (as); Lucky Thompson (ts); Jack Nimitz (bars); Billy Taylor (p); Charles Mingus (b); Charlie Persip (d); Quincy Jones (arr).   *NYC. September 19, 1956*
      BOO'S BLOOS   ABC-PARAMOUNT (Am) ABC149
      A SLEEPIN' BEE   "

Art Farmer, Bernie Glow, Ernie Royal, Joe Wilber (tp); Jimmy Cleveland, Urbie Green, Frank Rehank (tb); Phil Woods (as); Bunny Bardach, Lucky Thompson (ts); Jerome Richardson (fl, ts); Jack Nimitz (bars); Hank Jones (p); Paul Chambers (b); Charlie Persip (d); Quincy Jones (arr). *NYC. September 29, 1956*
      STOCKHOLM SWEETNIN'   ABC-PARAMOUNT (Am) ABC149
      WALKIN'   "
ABC149 = HMV (Eu) CLP1162 = Jasmine (Eu) JASM1035
Title: This is how I feel about jazz.

QUINCY JONES ALL STARS
Buddy Collette, Bill Perkins, Walter Benton (ts); Pepper Adams (bars); Carl Perkins (p); Leroy Vinnegar (b); Shelly Manne (d); Quincy Jones (arr).
                                                LA. February 25, 1957
      BRIGHT MOON   ABC-PARAMOUNT (Am) ABC186
      THE OOM IS BLUES   "
      BALLAD MEDLEY:
          What's new ts BP   "
          We'll be together again
             barPA   "
          Time on my hands tsBC   "
          You go to my head
             (rhythm only)   "
          Laura tsWB   "

QUINCY JONES ALL STARS

Benny Carter, Herb Geller, Charlie Mariano, Art Pepper (as); Lou Levy (p);
Red Mitchell (b); Shelly Manne (d); Jimmy Giuffre, Lennie Niehaus (arr).

LA. February 25, 1957

	BE MY GUEST aLN	ABC-PARAMOUNT (Am) ABC186
	DANCIN' PANTS aJG	,,
	KING'S ROAD BLUES aLN	,,

ABC186=HMV (Eu) CLP1157.

QUINCY JONES AND HIS ORCHESTRA

Ernie Royal, Harry Edison, Clark Terry (tp); Billy Byers, Jimmy Cleveland,
Urbie Green, Tom Mitchell (tb); Phil Woods (as); Jerome Richardson (as, ts, fl);
Budd Johnson, Sam Taylor (ts); Danny Bank (bars); Moe Weschler (p); Kenny
Burrell (g); Milt Hinton (b); Osie Johnson (d); Jimmy Crawford (percussion);
Quincy Jones (tp, arr). *NYC. February 9/10, 1959*

18126	TUXEDO JUNCTION	Mercury (Am) MG20444, SR60129
18127	SYNCOPATED CLOCK	,, ,,

Add Julius Watkins (frh). Sahib Shihab (bars), Patti Bown (p), Sam Woodyard
(d) replace Danny Bank, Moe Weschler and Osie Johnson.

NYC. March 9/10, 1959

18312	THE HUCKLEBUCK	Mercury (Am) MG21050, SR61050
18316	BLUES IN THE NIGHT	,, ,,
18318	AFTER HOURS	,, ,,

QUINCY JONES AND HIS ORCHESTRA

Ernie Royal, Harri Edison, Clark Terry, Joe Wilder (tp); Jimmy Cleveland,
Urbie Green, Quentin Jackson (tb); Melba Liston (tb, arr); Julius Watkins (frh);
Phil Woods, Frank Wess (as); Benny Golson, Jerome Richardson (ts); Danny
Bank (bars); Patti Bown (p); Kenny Burrell (g); Milt Hinton (b); Charlie Persip
(d); Nat Pierce, Al Cohn, Quincy Jones (arr). *NYC. May 26, 1959*

18642	MOANIN'	Mercury (Am) MG20444, SR60129

Joe Newman (tp), Zoot Sims (ts), Sahib Shihab (bars), Sam Woodyard (d)
replace Harry Edison, Jerome Richardson, Danny Bank and Charlie Persip.
Frank Wess doubles (fl). *NYC. May 27/28, 1959*

18643	HAPPY FACES	Mercury (Am) MG20444, SR60129
18644	ALONG CAME BETTY	,, ,,
18645	I REMEMBER CLIFFORD aNP	,, ,,
18646	WHISPER NOT	,, ,,
18647	THE GYPSY aML	,, ,,
18648	TICKLE TOE aAC	,, ,,

Harry Edison (tp), Jerome Richardson (ts), Les Spann (g), Don Lamond (d) replace Clark Terry, Benny Golson, Kenny Burrell and Sam Woodyard.

NYC. June 16, 1959

18716	A CHANGE OF PACE	Mercury (Am) MG20444, SR60129
18717	BIRTH OF A BAND	” ”

MG20444=Mercury (Eu) MMV14038, CMS18026, 125055MCL, 135055MCY, Fontana (Eu) 6430130
Title: Birth of a band.

QUINCY JONES AND HIS ORCHESTRA
(Collective personnel) Ernie Royal, Jimmy Maxwell, Art Farmer, Lee Morgan, Nick Travis, Lonnie Johnson (tp); Jimmy Cleveland, Frank Rehak, Urbie Green, Billy Byers (tb); Julius Watkins (frh); Phil Woods, Porter Kilbert (as); Budd Johnson (ts); Jerome Richardson (ts, fl); Sahib Shihab (bars); Patti Bown (p); Les Spann (g, fl); Buddy Catlett (b); Don Lamond (d); Ernie Wilkins, Bill Potts, Al Cohn, Ralph Burns (arr). *NYC, November 4/5/9, 1959*

19383	I HAVE NEVER SEEN SNOW aBP	Mercury (Am) MG20561, SR60221
19384	AIRMAIL SPECIAL aAC	” ”
19385	CHANT OF THE WEED aRB	” ”
19386	EVERYBODY'S BLUES aEW	” ”
19387	CHEROKEE aEW	” ”
19388	EESOM aBP	” ”
19389	LESTER LEAPS IN aEW	” ”
19390	CARAVAN aBP	” ”
19391	THEY SAY IT'S WONDERFUL aAC	” ”
19392	GHANA aEW	” ”

MG20561=Mercury (Eu) MMC14046, CMS18031, EmArcy (Eu) 6336705
Title: The great wide world of Quincy Jones.

QUINCY JONES AND HIS ORCHESTRA
Lonnie Johnson, Benny Bailey, Clark Terry, Floyd Stadifer, (tp); Jimmy Cleveland, Ake Persson, Melba Liston, Quentin Jackson (tb); Phil Woods, Porter Kilbert (as); Budd Johnson, Jerome Richardson (ts); Sahib Shihab (bars); Patti Bown (p); Les Spann (g, fl); Buddy Catlett (b); Joe Harris (d); Quincy Jones (arr). *Paris. France, February 27, 1960*

20042	LOVE IS HERE TO STAY	Mercury (Am) MG20612, SR60612
20043	MOONGLOW	” ”
20044	TROUBLE IN MIND	” ”

As previous. *Paris. France, February 29, 1960*

20044	CHINESE CHECKERS	Mercury (Am) MG20612, SR60612

As Previous. *Paris. France, April 21, 1960*

20047	A SUNDAY KIND OF LOVE	Mercury (Am) MG20612, SR60612
20048	THE MIDNIGHT SUN WILL NEVER SET	” ”

QUINCY JONES AND HIS ORCHESTRA

Benny Bailey, Clyde Reasinger, Freddie Hubbard, Jerry Kail (tp); Melba Liston, Curtis Fuller, Quentin Jackson, Wayne Andre (tb); Phil Woods, Joe Lopez (as); Oliver Nelson, Jerome Richardson (ts); Sahib Shihab (bars); Patti Bown (p); Les Spann (g, fl); Buddy Catlett (b); Stu Martin (d), Quincy Jones (arr).

NYC. October 19, 1960

20570	G'WAN TRAIN	Mercury (Am) MG20612, SR60612	
20572	YOU TURNED THE TABLES ON ME	"	"
20573	TONE POEM	"	"
20578	PLEASINGLY PLUMP	"	"

MG20612 = Mercury (Eu) MMC14080, CMS18055
Title: I dig dancers

QUINCY JONES AND HIS ORCHESTRA

(Partial personnel) Bennie Bailey, Ernie Royal (tp); Clarke Terry (flh); Curtis Fuller (tb); Julius Watkins (frh); Phil Woods (as); Eric Dixon, Jerome Richardson, (ts, fl); Sahib Shihab (bars, fl); Don Elliott (vbs, percussion); Quincy Jones (arr).   *NYC. January 24, 1961*

20838	STRIKE UP THE BAND (USA)	Mercury (Am) PPS2014, SR6014

As previous.   *NYC. February 21, 1961*

20839	MACK THE KNIFE (GERMANY)	Mercury (Am) PPS2014, SR6014	
20840	UNDER PARIS SKIES (FRANCE)	"	"
20841	SWEDISH WARMLAND (SWEDEN)	"	"
20842	DANNY BOY (IRELAND)	"	"

As previous, add Tito Puente, Potato Valdez, Mike Olatunji (percussion).

NYC. February 23, 1961

20843	BAIA (BRAZIL)	Mercury (Am) PPS2014, SR6014	
20844	RICO VACILION (CUBA)	"	"
20845	MANOLETE DE ESPANA (SPAIN)	"	"
20846	AFRICANA (AFRICA)	"	"

Omit added percussion.   *NYC. February 27, 1961*

20847	MEADOWLANDS (RUSSIA)	Mercury (Am) PPS2014, SR6014	
20848	COME BACK TO SORRENTO (ITALY)	"	"
20849	HOT SAKE (JAPAN)	"	"

All titles, except Danny boy, on Mercury (Eu) MMC14098, CMS18064 title: Around the world and Mercury (Eu) SMWL30003 title: Travellin'.

PEGGY LEE with QUINCY JONES AND HIS ORCHESTRA

(Collective personnel) Frank Beach, Bob Fowler, Conrad Gozzo, Manny Klein, Al Porcino, Jack Sheldon (tp); Vern Friley, Frank Rosolino, Lew McGreary, Bob Knight, (tb); Benny Carter (as, arr); Bill Green (as); Plas Johnson, Bill Perkins (ts); Jack Nimitz (bars); Lou Levey, Jimmy Rowles (p); Dennis Budimir (g); Max Bennett (b); Stan Levey (d); Chano Pozo (conga, bongo); Quincy Jones (arr).

LA. April 14/15, 1961

BOSTON BEANS	Capitol (Am) T1671, ST1671
KANSAS CITY BLUES	" "
BASIN STREET BLUES	" "
GOING TO CHICAGO BLUES	" "
NEW YORK CITY BLUES	" "
LOS ANGELES BLUES	" "
SAN FRANSISCO BLUES aBC	" "
I LOST MY SUGAR IN SALT	
LAKE CITY	" "
ST. LOUIS BLUES	" "
FISHERMAN'S WHARF	" "
THE TRAIN BLUES	" "
THE GREEN BELT BLUES	" "
ORANGE BLUES	" "

Title: Blues Cross Country, ST1671 = Capitol (Eu) 1552941

QUINCY JONES AND HIS ORCHESTRA

Jimmy Maxwell, Jimmy Nottingham, Joe Newman, John Bello (tp); Curtis Fuller, Britt Woodman, Melba Liston, Paul Faulise (tb); Julius Watkins (frh); Phil Woods, Joe Lopez (as); Eric Dixon, Jerome Richardson (ts, fl); Pat Patrick (bars); Patti Bown (p); Les Spann (g, fl); Art Davis (d); Stu Martin (d); Quincy Jones (arr). *Newport Jazz Festival. July 3, 1961*

21119	MEET B.B.	Mercury (Am) MG20653, SR60653
21120	G'WAN TRAIN	" "
21121	EVENING IN PARIS	" "
21122	BANJA LIKO	" "
21123	LESTER LEAPS IN	" "
21124	BOY IN THE TREE	" "
21125	AIRMAIL SPECIAL	" "

MG20653 = Mercury (Eu) 125009MCL

QUINCY JONES AND HIS ORCHESTRA

Jerry Kail, Clyde Reasinger, Clark Terry, Joe Newman (tp); Billy Byers, Melba Liston, Paul Faulise (tb); Julius Watkins (frh); Phil Woods (as); Eric Dixon (ts, fl); Jerome Richardson (ts, bars, fl); Bobby Scott (p); Buddy Catlett (b); Stu Martin (d); Quincy Jones (arr). *NYC. November 29, 1961*

FOR LENA AND LENNIE	Impulse (Am) A11, AS11
THE TWITCH	" "

Thad Jones, Al Derisi, Freddie Hubbard, Snooky Young (tp); Rod Levitt, Melba Liston, Billy Byers, Paul Faulise (tb); Julius Watkins (frh); Phil Woods, Frank Wess (as), Eric Dixon (ts, fl); Oliver Nelson (ts); Jerome Richardson (bars); Patti Bown (p); Milt Hinton (b); Bill English (d); Quincy Jones (arr).

		NYC. December 18, 1961
	HARD SOCK DANCE	Impulse (Am) A11, AS11
	LITTLE KAREN	" "
	ROBOT PORTRAIT	" "

QUINCY JONES AND HIS ORCHESTRA
Thad Jones, Ernie Royal, Joe Newman, Snooky Young (tp); Curtis Fuller, Melba Listion, Billy Byers, Paul Faulise, Tom Mitchell (tb); Julius Watkins, Jimmy Buffington, Earl Chapin, Ray Alonge (frh); Harvey Phillips (tu); Phil Woods (as); Oliver Nelson (ts); Jerome Richardson (ts, bars, fl); Patti Bown (p); Milt Hinton (b); Osie Johnson (d); Gloria Agostini (harp); Quincy Jones (arr).

		NYC. December 22, 1961
	QUINTESSENCE	Impulse (Am) A11, AS11
	INVITATION	" "
	STRAIGHT/NO CHASER	" "

AS11=HMV (Eu) CLP1581, SCD1462, Jasmine (Eu) JAS79
Title: The Quintessence

Personnel unknown.   *NYC. June 15, 1962*
25135	A TASTE OF HONEY	Mercury (Am) MG20799, SR60799
25138	SERMONETTE	Mercury (Am) MG21050, SR61050

See November 1964 and March/August 1965 for further titles on MG21050

QUINCY JONES AND HIS ORCHESTRA
Big band instrumentation of tps, tbs, frh, reeds and rhythm. including Clark Terry (tp); Phil Woods (as); Roland Kirk (reeds); Paul Gonsalves (ts);? Jerome Richardson (reeds, fl); Lalo Schifrin (p); Jim Hall (g); Chris White (b); Rudy Collins (d); Jose Paula, Carlos Gomez, Jack Del Rio (percussion); Quincy Jones (arr).   *NYC. August 13, 1962*
22191	SOUL BOSSA NOVA	Mercury (Am) MG20751, SR60751

		NYC. September 4, 1962
22136	SAMBA DE UNA NOTA (One	
	note samba)	Mercury (Am) MG20751, SR60751
22137	BOOGIE BOSSA NOVA	" "
22138	MANHA DE CARNAVAL	" "

		NYC. September 7, 1962
22139	LALO'S BOSSA NOVA	Mercury (Am) MG20751, SR60751
22140	ON THE STREET WHERE YOU LIVE	" "
22142	SERENATA	" "

22143   DESAFINADO   Mercury (Am) MG20751, SR60751
22144   CHEGA DE SAUDADE   "   "

NYC. September 12, 1961
22190   SE E TARDE ME PARDOA   Mercury (Am) MG20751, SR60751
MG20751 = Mercury (Eu) MMC14124, CMS18080, 125258MCL, 814224-1
Title: Big band bossa nova

QUINCY JONES AND HIS ORCHESTRA
(Collective personnel) Joe Newman, Clark Terry, Ernie Royal, Snookie Young, Jimmy Nottingham, Al DeDerisi (tp); Billy Byers, Paul Faulise, Jimmy Cleveland, Quentin Jackson, Kai Winding, Thomas Mitchell, Sonny Russo, Melba Liston (tb); Julius Watkins, James Buffington, Ray Alonge, Bob Northern, Earl Chaplin, Paul Ingraham, Fred Klein, Willie Ruff (frh); Bill Stanley, James McAllister (tu); James Moody, Walt Levinsky, Al Cohn, Frank Wess, Roland Kirk, Budd Johnson, Seldon Powell, Romeo Penque, Jerome Richardson, Zoot Sims (saxs, fl); Lalo Schifrin, Bobby Scott, Patti Bown (p, organ); Kenny Burrell, Jim Hall, Wayne Wright, Sam Herman (g); Milt Hinton, Art Davis, George Duvivier, Ben Tucker, Major Holley, Chris White (b); Osie Johnson, Rudy Collins, Ed Shaughnessy (d); James Johnson (tymps); Charles McCoy (tymps, harmonica); Carlos Gomez, Jack del Rio, Jose Paula, Bill Costa, George Devins (percussion); Quincy Jones (arr).   *NYC. April 9, 1963*
22890   BACK AT THE CHICKEN SHACK   Mercury (Am) MG20799, SR20799
22891   COMIN' HOME BABY   "   "
22892   GRAVY WALTZ   "   "

As previous.   *NYC. April 10, 1963*
22894   EXODUS   Mercury (Am) MG20799, SR20799
22895   JIVE SAMBA   "   "
22896   WALK ON THE WILD SIDE   "   "

As previous.   *NYC. April 11, 1963*
22897   TAKE FIVE   Mercury (Am) MG20799, SR20799
22898   CAST YOU FATE TO THE WIND   "   "
22899   BOSA NOVA U.S.A.   "   "
22900   WATERMELON MAN   "   "
MG20799 = Mercury (Eu) MMC14128, 12531MCL, 13531MCY

QUINCY JONES AND HIS ORCHESTRA
Ernie Royal (tp); Billy Byers (tb); Phil Woods (as); Zoot Sims (ts); Jerome Richardson, Wally Kane (saxs,fl); Gary Burton (vbs); Bobby Scott (p); Toots Thielmans (g, harmonica); Major Holley, Milt Hinton (b); Osie Johnson (d); Quincy Jones (arr).   *NYC. February 5, 1964*
31074   ODD BALL   Mercury (Am) MG20863, SR60863
31075   BIRD BRAIN   "   "
31076   PINK PANTHER   "   "
31077   SOLDIER IN THE RAIN   "   "

Clark Terry, Snooky Young, Jimmy Maxwell, Ernie Royal (tp); Dick Hixon, Urbie Green, Billy Byers, Quentin Jackson, Tony Studd (tb); Jimmy Buffington, Tony Miranda, Bob Northern, Ray Alonge (frh); Harvey Phillips (tu); Jerome Richardson, Stan Webb, Roland Kirk (saxs, fl); Gary Burton (vbs); Bobby Scott (p); Mundell Lowe (g); Milt Hinton (b); Osie Johnson (d); Marty Grupp (percussion); Margaretha Ross (harp); Quincy Jones (arr).   *NYC. same date*

31078	DAYS OF WINE AND ROSES	Mercury (Am) MG20863, SR60863	
31079	MOON RIVER	”	”
31080	DREAMSVILLE	”	”
31081	(I love you) DON'T YOU FORGET IT	”	”

John Bellow, Snooky Young, Jimmy Maxwell, Ernie Royal (tp); Dick Hixon, Urbie Green, Billy Byers, Quentin Jackson, Tony Studd (tb); Jerome Richardson, Roland Kirk, Phil Woods, Seldon Powell, Romeo Penque, George Berg (saxs, fl); Gary Burton (vbs); Bobby Scott (p); Vincent Bell (g); Major Holley, Milt Hinton (b); Osie Johnson (d); Phil Kraus (percussion); Quincy Jones (arr).
NYC. February 6, 1964

31082	BABY ELEPHANT WALK	Mercury (Am) MG20863, SR60863	
31083	CHARADE	”	”
31084	MR LUCKY	”	”
31085	PETER GUNN	”	”

MG20863=Mercury (Eu) 125917MCL, 125917MCY, SMCL20016
Title: Quincy Jones explores the music of Henry Mancini

QUINCY JONES AND HIS ORCHESTRA
Jim Buffington, Morris Secon (frh); Eddie Davis, Jerome Richardson, George Dessinger, Bill Saplin, Stan Webb (saxs); Don Elliott (marimba, vbs, vcl); Bobby Scott (p); Jim Hall (g); Milt Hinton, Art Davis (b); Ed Shaughnessy (d); strings; Margaret Ross (harp); Quincy Jones (arr).   *NYC. June   1964*

32405	GOLDEN BOY THEME	Mercury (Am) MG20938, SR60938	
32406	SEAWEED vDE	”	”

John Frosk, Joe Newman, Dick Hurwitz, Freddie Hubbard (tp); Billy Byers, Al Gray, Quentin Jackson, Paul Faulise, Bill Watrous (tb); Jim Buffington, Morris Secon (frh); Phil Woods (as); Jerome Richardson (as, sop, flu); Frank Foster, Eddie Davis (ts); Cecil Payne (bars); strings; Bobby Scott (p); Jim Hall (g); Bob Cranshaw (b); Grady Tate (d); Quincy Jones (arr).   *NYC. September 15, 1964*

33954	A HARD DAY'S NIGHT	Mercury (Am) MG20938, SR60938	
33955	SIDEWINDER	”	”
33956	THE MIDNIGHT SUN WILL NEVER SET	”	”
33957	GOLDEN BOY THEME (omit strings)	”	”
33958	SOUL SERENADE	”	”
33959	DJANGO	”	”
33960	GOLDEN BOY	”	”
33961	THE WITCHING HOUR	”	”

MG20938=Mercury (Eu) 135962MCY, MCL20047, SMCL20047
Title: Golden boy

FRANK SINATRA with COUNT BASIE AND HIS ORCHESTRA
Al Porcino, Don Rader, Wallace Davenport, Al Aarons, Sonnt Cohn, Harry Edison (tp); Henry Coker, Grover Mitchell, Bill Hughes, Henderson Chambers, Ken Schroyer (tb); Marshall Royal, Frank Wess (as); Frank Foster, Eric Dixon (ts); Charlie Fowlkes (bars); Emil Richards (vbs); Count Basie (p); Freddie Green (g); Buddy Catlett (b); Sonny Payne (d); Frank Sinatra (vcl); Quincy Jones (arr, conductor).   *LA. June 9, 1964*

2809	THE BEST IS YET TO COME	Reprise (Am) FS1012,	(Eu) K44004
2810	I WANNA BE AROUND	"	"
2811	I BELIEVE IN YOU	"	"
2812	FLY ME TO THE MOON	"	"

Same as June 9 except string section added.   *LA. June 10, 1964*

2814	HELLO DOLLY	Reprise (Am) FS1012,	(Eu) K44004
2815	THE GOOD LIFE	"	"
2816	I WISH YOU LOVE	"	"

Same as June 10.   *LA. June 12, 1964*

2817	I CAN'T STOP LOVING YOU	Reprise (Am) FS1012,	(Eu) K44004
2818	MORE	"	"
2819	WIVES AND LOVERS	"	"

Title: It might as well be swing

QUINCY JONES AND HIS ORCHESTRA
Big band instrumentation, personnell unknown.   *NYC. November 27, 1964*

34109	BLUES FOR TRUMPET AND KOTO	Mercury (Am) MG21050, SR61050

As previous.   *NYC. March 10, 1965*

35079	NONSTOP TO BRAZIL	Mercury (Am) MG21050, SR61050
35080	THE GENTLE RAIN	" "

As previous.   *NYC. August 5, 1965*

36751	WHAT'S NEW PUSSYCAT	Mercury (Am) MG21050, SR61050
36752	WALK IN THE BLACK FOREST	" "
36753	THE 'IN' CROWD	" "
36754	I CAN'T GET NO SATISFACTION	" "

MG21050=Mercury (Eu) SMCL20073, 135986MCY
Title: Plays for pussycats

QUINCY JONES AND HIS ORCHESTRA
Bobby Bryant, (tp); Urbie Green, Ken Shroyer (tb); Jackie Kelso (as); Plas Johnson (ts); Jewel Grant (as, bars); Mike Rubini, Ray Charles (p, organ); Rene Hall, Arthur Knight (g); Carol Kay (b); Grady Tate (d); Gary Coleman (percussion); Quincy Jones (arr, conductor).   *LA. November 24, 1965*

37006	FEVER	Mercury (Am) MG21063, SR61063
37007	BABY CAKES	" "

Joe Newman (tp); Jerome Richardson (ts); Bobby Scott (p, conductor); Ben Tucker (b); Grady Tate (d); Ray Barretto (percussion); Quincy Jones (arr).

NYC. November 26, 1965

37193	BOSS BIRD	Mercury (Am) MG21063, SR61063	
37194	I HEAR A RHAPSODY	"	"
37195	HARLEM NOCTURNE	"	"
37196	HANG ON SLOOPY	"	"

Same as November 24, 1965
LA. November 27, 1965

37200	'AINT THAT PECULIAR	Mercury (Am) MG21063, SR61063	
37201	SOMETHING ABOUT YOU	"	"
37202	I GOT YOU	"	"
37203	PAPA'S GOT A BRAND NEW BAG	"	"
37204	A LOVER'S CONCERTO	"	"
37205	MOHAIR SAM	"	"

MG21063 = Mercury (Eu) 13599MCY, MCL20078, SMCL20078
Title: Got a brand new bag

QUINCY JONES AND HIS ORCHESTRA

Freddie Hubbard, Lloyh Michels, Marvin Stamm, Richard Williams (tp, flh); Jimmy Cleveland, J.J. Johnson, Alan Ralph, Tony Studd (tb); Roland Kirk, Hubert Laws, Jerome Richardson, Joel Kaye (saxs, fl); Paul Griffin (p); Eric Gale (g); Ray Brown (b); Grady Tate (d); Hilda Harris, Marilyn Jackson, Valerie Simpson, Martha Stewart (vcl); Quincy Jones (arr).   *NJ. June 18, 1969*

KILLER JOE	A & M (Am) SP3023, CS3023	

John Frosk, Snooky Young (tp, flh), George Jeffers, Kai Winding (tb); Bob James (electric p, arr) replace Lloyd Michels, Richard Williams, J.J. Johnson, Alan Ralph and Paul Griffin. Add Toots Thielmans (g, harmonica).

NJ. June 19, 1969

DEAD END	A & M (Am) SP3023, CS3023	
WALKING IN SPACE	"	"
I NEVER TOLD YOU aBJ	"	"

Lloyd Michels (tp, flh); Alan Ralph, J.J. Johnson (tb); Bernard Purdie (d) replace Snooky Young, George Jeffers, Kai Winding and Grady Tate. Omit Toots Thielmans add Norman Purdie (tb).   *same date*

OH HAPPY DAY	A & M (Am) SP3023, CS3023	

Add Chuck Rainey (amplified b)   *same date*

LOVE AN PEACE	A & M (Am) SP3023, CS3023	

SP3023 = A & M (Eu) AMLS961
Title: Walking in Space

QUINCY JONES AND HIS ORCHESTRA

Freddie Hubbard, Snooky Young, Marvin Stamm, Ernie Royal, Danny Moore (tp, flh); Wayne Andre, Al Grey, Benny Powell, Tony Studd (tb); Hubert Laws, Jerome Richardson, Danny Bank (saxs, fl); Toots Thielmans (g, harmonica, whistling); Milt Jackson (vbs); Herbie Hancock, Bob James, Bobby Scott (electric p, p); Eric Gale (g); Major Holley (b, vcl); Ray Brown (b); Grady Tate (d); Warren Smith, Jimmy Johnson (percussion); Valerie Simpson (vcl); vocal group; Quincy Jones (arr).   *NJ. March 25, 26, 1970*

BRIDGE OVER TROUBLED WATERS	A & M (Am) SP3030, CS3030	
WALKIN'	"	"
HUMMIN'	"	"

Add Don Elliott (bass marimba), Ron Carter and Richard Davis (b).

NJ. May 12, 1970

GULA MATARI	A & M (Am) SP3030, CS3030

SP3030=A & M (Eu) AMLS992
Title: Gula Matari

From this point on most personnel listings are collective. Also the precise venue and date of recording are difficult to pinpoint due to the extensive use of multi-tracking and over-dubbing in different locations.

QUINCY JONES AND HIS ORCHESTRA

(Collective personnel) Freddie Hubbard, Snooky Young, Marvin Stamm, Ernie Royal, Joe Newman, Buddy Childers (tp, flh); Wayne Andre, Garnett, Brown, Dick Hixon, Alan Ralph, Tony Studd (tb); Jerome Richardson (ts, ss); Hubert Laws (ts, fl); Pete Christlieb (ts); Milt Jackson (vbs); Harry Lookofsky (multi tracked violins); Bobby Scott (p); Bob James (fender rhodes p); Jackie Byard (fender p); Monty Alexander (tack, p); Joe Sample (fender p); Dick Hyman (electric harpsichord, p); Jimmy Smith (organ); Paul Beaver, Edd Kalehoff (moog synthesizer); Toots Thielmans (harmonica, whistler, g); Ray Brown (b); Chuck Rainey, Carole Kaye (fender b); Grady Tate, Paul Humphries (d); George Devens, Larry Bunker (percussion); Valerie Simpson, Maretha Steward, Marilyn Jackson, Barbara Massey, Joshie Armstead, Bill Cosby (vcl); Marty Paich (arr); Quincy Jones (vcl, arr).   *NYC.   1971*

SMACKWATER JACK vQJ	A & M (Am) SP3037, CS3037	
CAST YOUR FATE TO THE WIND	"	"
INRONSIDE	"	"
WHAT'S GOING ON? vVS, QJ	"	"
THEME FROM "THE ANDERSON TAPES" aMP	"	"
BROWN BALLAD	"	"
HIKKY-BURR vBC	"	"
GUITAR BLUES ODYSSEY,		
FROM ROOTS TO FRUITS	"	"

Note: Sleeve note gives recording location as A & M studios New York City but the above personnel includes many Los Angeles based musicians.
SP3037=A & M (Eu) AMLS63037
Title: Smackwater Jack

QUINCY JONES AND HIS ORCHESTRA

big band instrumentation including Cat Anderson (tp); Phil Woods (as); Hubert Laws (sax, fl); Ernie Watts (saxs); Jerome Richardson (saxs, ss); Tom Morgan (harmonica); Toots Thielmans (harmonica, g, whistler); Eddie Louis (organ); Bob James, Dave Grusin (electric p); Dennis Budimir (g); Valerie Simpson (vcl); Quincy Jones (vcl, arr).   NYC & LA   1973

SUMMER IN THE CITY vVS	A & M (Am) SP3041, CS3041	
TRIBUTE TO A.F.-RO		
Daydreaming vVS, QJ; First time ever I saw your face vVS, QJ	"	"
LOVE THEME FROM "THE GETAWAY"	"	"
YOU'VE GOT IT BAD GIRL vQJ	"	"
SUPERSTITION vQJ	"	"
MANTECA	"	"
THEME FROM "SANFORD AND SON"	"	"
CHUMP CHANGE	"	"

SP3041 = A & M (Eu) AMLS63041
Title: You've got it bad girl

QUINCY JONES AND HIS ORCHESTRA

Chuck Findley (tp); Frank Rosolino (tb); Hubert Laws, Jerome Richardson (saxs, fl); Clifford Soloman, Pete Christlieb (saxs); Tom Morgan (harmonica); Herbie Hancock (rhodes fender piano, arp odyssey); Richard Tee, Bob Jamerson (electric p); Billy Preston (arp soloist, organ); Mike Melbain (synthesizer); Robert Margouleff, Malcolm Cecil (arp synthesizer prgramming); Phil Upchurch, Arthur Adams, Dennis Coffee, Eric Gale, Wah Wah Watson, David T. Walker (g); Chuck Rainey, Melvin Dunlap, Max Bennett (b); Paul Humphrey, Bernard Purdie, Grady Tate (d); Bobby Hall (percussion, conga, cow bells, rhythm logs, B&D 1962 Buick break drums); Leon Ware, Minnie Riperton, Tommy Bahler, Joe Greene, Jesse Kirkland, Jim Gilstrap, Carolyn Willis, Myra Mathews (vcl); Quincy Jones (vcl, arr).   NYC & LA   1974

BODY HEAT	A & M (Am) SP3617, CS3617	
SOUL SAGA (Ballad of the Buffalo soldier)	"	"
EVERYTHING MUST CHANGE	"	"
BOOGIE JOE (The grinder)	"	"
EVERYTHING MUST CHANGE-REPRISAL	"	"
ONE TRACK MIND	"	"
JUST A MAN	"	"
ALONG CAME BETTY	"	"
IF I EVER LOSE THIS HEAVEN vMR	"	"

Title: Body heat

QUINCY JONES AND HIS ORCHESTRA

Bill Lamb, Chuck Findley, Tom Bahler (tp); Frank Rosolino, George Bohanon (tb); Ernie Krivda, Jerome Richardson, Sahib Shihab (saxs, fl); Hubert Laws (fl)-1; Don Grusin, Dave Grusin, Jerry Peters (keyboards); Mike Melvoin (keyboards)-1; Wah Wah Watson, (g, vcl); George Johnson (g); Toots Thielmans (g)-2; Dennis Budimir (g)-3; Louis Johnson (b); Chuck Rainey (b)-2; Max Bennet (b)-1; Harvey Mason (d); Grady Tate (d)-2; Ralph McDonald (percussion); Ian Underwood (synthesizer programming); Tommy Morgan (bass harmonica)-3; Minnie Riperton (vcl)-1; Tom Bahler, Paulette McWilliams, Jim Gilstrap, Joe Greene, Jesse Kirkland, Myrna Matthews, Carolyn Willis, Leon Ware, The Watts Prophets (vcl); Quincy Jones (keyboards, tp, vcl, arr).

	NYC & LA	1975
IS IT LOVE THAT WE'RE MISSING	A & M (Am) SP4526,	CS4526
PARANOID	"	"
MELLOW MADNESS	"	"
BEAUTIFUL BLACK GIRL	"	"
LISTEN (What is it)	"	"
JUST A LITTLE TASTE OF ME -3	"	"
MY CHERIE AMOUR -1	"	"
TRYIN' TO FIND OUT ABOUT YOU	"	"
CRY BABY	"	"
BLUESETTE -2	"	"

SP4526=A & M (Eu) AMLH64526
Title: Mellow Madness

QUINCY JONES AND HIS ORCHESTRA

(Collective personnel) Cat Anderson, Tom Bahler, Bobby Bryant, Buddy Childers, Chuck Findley, John Frosk, Freddie Hubbard, Lloyd Michales, Danny Moore, Joe Newman, Ernie Royal, Marvin Stamm, Richard Williams, Snooky Young (tp); Wayne Andre, Garnett Brown, Jimmy Cleveland, Al Grey, Dick Hixon, J.J. Johnson, Benny Powell, George Jeffers, Frank Rosolino, Alan Ralph, Tony Studd, Kai Winding (tb); Pepper Adams, Danny Bank, Pete Christlieb, Roland Kirk, Joel Kaye, Hubert Laws, Jerome Richardson, Sahib Shihab, Clifford Solomon, Phil Woods (saxs, fl); strings; Milt Jackson (vbs); Stevie Wonder (harmonica); Toots Thielmans (harmonica, g); Paul Beaver, Malcolm Cecil, George Duke, Dave Grusin, Paul Griffin, Herbie Hancock, Bob James, Edd Kalehoff, Eddie Louis, Robert Margouleff, Billy Preston, Bobby Scott, Richard Tee, Michael Boddicker (keyboards, synthesizers); Eric Gale, George Johnson, Louis Johnson, David T. Walker, Wah Wah Watson (g); Ray Brown, Stanley Clarke, Ron Carter, Richard Davis, Major Holley, Louis Johnson, Carol Kaye, Chuck Rainey, James Jamerson, Aphonso Johnson (b); Billy Cobham, Paul Humphries, Harvery Mason, Grady Tate, James Gadson (d); Eddie Brown, George Devens, Don Elliot, Bobbye Hall Porter, Ralph McDonald, Harvey Mason, Warren Smith (percussion); Bruce Fisher, Joe Greene, Jim Gilstrap, Hilda Harris, Marilyn Jackson, George Johnson, Louis Johnson, Al Jarreau, Jesse Kirkland, Barbara Massey, Myrna Matthews, Minnie Riperton, Valerie Simpson, Maeretha Stewart, Stairsteps, Carolyn Willis, Leon Ware, Sherwood Sledge, David Pridgen, Rodney Armstrong, Mortonette Jenkins (vcl); Charles May (vcl, arr); Johnny Mandel (arr); Quincy Jones (vcl, tp, arr).

	LA. May	1976
I HEARD THAT!	A & M (Am) SP3705,	CS3705
THINGS COULD BE WORSE FOR ME	"	"

WHAT GOOD IS A SONG	,,	,,
YOU HAVE TO DO IT YOURSELF	,,	,,
THERE'S A TRAIN LEAVIN'	,,	,,
MIDNIGHT SOUL PATROL	,,	,,
BROWN SOFT SHOE	,,	,,
SUPERSTITION (1973)	,,	,,
SUMMER IN THE CITY (1973)	,,	,,
IS IT LOVE THAT WE'RE MISSIN' (1975)	,,	,,
BODY HEAT (1974)	,,	,,
IF I EVER LOSE THIS HEAVEN (1974)	,,	,,
KILLER JOE (1969)	,,	,,
GULA MATARI (1970)	,,	,,
THEME FROM "THE ANDERSON TAPES" (1971)	,,	,,
WALKING IN SPACE (1969)	,,	,,

Note: dates in brackets are recording dates, this is a double LP.

QUINCY JONES AND HIS ORCHESTRA

John Faddis, Virgil Jones (tp); Alan Ralph (bass tb); George Young, David Tofoni, Harold Vick, Howard Johnson (saxs, fl). _NYC._ _1978_

Chuck Findley, Snooky Young, Oscar Brashear, Bill Lamb (tp); Chauncy Welch, Robert Payne, Jimmy Cleveland, Donald Waldrup, Bill Watrous, Charlie Loper (tb); Henry Sigismonti, David Duke, Sidney Muldrow, Arthur Maebe, Aubrey Bouth (frh); Tommy Johnson, Roger Bobo (tu); Hubert Laws, Bud Shank, Bill Perkins, Jerome Richardson, Buddy Collette (saxs, fl); Gayle Levant (harp); Michael Boddicker (synthesizer, vocordor); strings. _LA._ _1978_

Tom Bahler, Patti Austin, Gwen Guthrie, Lani Groves, Vivian Cherry, Yolanda McCullough, Luther Vandross, Zach Sanders, Bill Eaton, Frank Floyd (vcl group). _NYC._ _1978_

Richard Tee (p, organ, synthesizer keyboard bass); Eric Gale (g); Anthony Jackson (b); Steve Gadd (d); Ralph McDonald (percussion).
NYC & LA _1978_

Nick Ashford, Valerie Simpson (vcl)-1; Charles May (vcl)-2; Tom Scott (lyricon)-3; Michael Brecker (ts)-4; Herbie Hancock (electric p)-5; David T. Walker (g)-6; Wah Wah Watson (g)-7; Johnny Mandel, Leon Pendarvis, Sy Johnson, Quincy Jones (arr).

STUFF LIKE THAT -1,6	A & M (Am) SP4685, CS4685
I'M GONNA MISS YOU IN	
THE MORNING vPA, LV, -3	,, ,,
LOVE, I NEVER HAD IT SO GOOD vPA, -2, 4	,, ,,
TELL ME A BEDTIME STORY -5	,, ,,
LOVE ME BY NAME vPA, -5	,, ,,
SUPERWOMAN vPA, -3, 5	,, ,,
TAKIN' IT TO THE STREETS vLV, GG, -4, 7	,, ,,

SP4685 = A & M (Eu) AMLH64685
Title: Sounds . . . and stuff like that!

QUINCY JONES AND HIS ORCHESTRA

Jerry Hey (tp, arr); Chuck Findley (tp); Bill Reichenbach (tb); Kim Hutchcroft, Ernie Watts, Larry Williams (saxs, fl); David Wolinski (clarinet, mini moog synthesizer, programming, Yamaha CS-80 synthesizer bass); Ian Underwood (synthesizer, programming); Greg Phillinganes (electric p, synthesizer, hand claps); Craig Hundley (beam-microtonal tubulons); Michael Boddicker (synthesizer, vocoder); Herbie Hancock (electric p); Stevie Wonder (Yamaha CS-80 synthesizer, arr); Robbie Buchanan (p, string synthesizer); David Foster (p, electric p); Toots Thielmans (g, harmonica, whistler); Steve Lukather (g); Louis Johnson, Abraham Laborie (b, hand claps); John Robinson (d, hand claps); Paulinho DaCosta (percussion, mouth percussion); Lenny Castro (hand claps); Charles May, Patti Austin, Tom Bahler, Jim Gilstrap, James Ingram, Michael Jackson, Syretta Wright, Lalomie Washburn, Yvonne Lewis, Casey Cysick (vcl, vcl group); Rod Temperton, Johnny Mandel (arr); Quincy Jones (vcl, arr, producer). *LA.* *1982*

AI NO CORRIDA aQJ, JH, vCM	A & M (Am) EC7054, (Eu) AMLK63721	
THE DUDE aJH, RT, QJ, vJI	,,	,,
JUST ONCE aJH, JM, QJ, vJI	,,	,,
BETCHA' WOULDN'T HURT ME aJH, SW, QJ, vPA	,,	,,
SOMETHIN' SPECIAL aJH, RT, vPA	,,	,,
RAZZMATAZZ aJH, RT, QJ, vPA	,,	,,
ONE HUNDRED WAYS aJH, JM, QJ, vJI	,,	,,
VELAS aJM, QJ	,,	,,
TURN ON THE ACTION JH, RT, vPA	,,	,,

Title: The Dude

MICHAEL JACKSON with QUINCY JONES ORCHESTRA

Jerry Hey (tp, flh), arr); Gary Grant (tp, flh); Bill Reichenbach (tb); Larry Williams (saxs, fl); Greg Phillinganes (rhodes synthesizer, keyboards, synthesizer programming, hand claps); Bill Wolfer (keyboards, synthesizer, synthesizer programming); Michael Boddicker (synthesizer, emulator, vocodor); David Paich (synthesizer, p, arr); David Foster (synthesizer, arr); Brian Banks (synthesizer); Rod Temperton (synthesizer, arr); Greg Smith (synthesizer, synergy); Steve Porcaro (synthesizer, programming, arr); Tom Bahler (synclavier); James Ingram (portasound keyboard, arr, hand claps, vcl); strings cond. by Jeremey Lubbock; David Williams, Dean Parks, Eddie Van Halen, Paul Jackson (g); Steve Lukather (g, electric b, arr); Louis Johnson (b, hand claps); Ndugu Chancler, Jeff Porcaro (d); Paulinho deCosta (percussion); Nelson Hayes (bathroom stomp board); Steven Ray (bathroom stomp board, hand claps); Julia Waters, Maxine Waters, Oren Waters, Bunny Hull, Becky Lopez, Paul

McCartney (vcl); Vincent Price (voice 'rap'); Michael Jackson (vcl, arr, percussion, hand claps, bathroom stomp board); Quincy Jones (arr, producer).

LA. *1982*

BEAT IT	Epic (Am) QE-38112,	(Eu) EPC85930
BILLIE JEAN	"	"
HUMAN NATURE	"	"
P.Y.T. (Pretty young thing)	"	"
THE LADY IN MY LIFE	"	"
WANNA BE STARTIN' SOMETHIN'	"	"
BABY BE MINE	"	"
THE GIRL IS MINE	"	"
THRILLER	"	"

Title: Thriller

FRANK SINATRA with QUINCY JONES ORCHESTRA
Alan Rubin, Joe Newman, Randy Brecker, Lou Soloff, John Faddis (tp); Wayne Andre, Urbie Green, Dave Taylor, Benny Powell (tb); George Young, Frank Wess, Frank Foster, Michael Brecker, Ron Cuber (reeds); Peter Gordon, John Clark, Jerry Peel (frh); Tony Price (tuba); Margaret Ross (harp); Bob James, Joe Parnello, Sy Johnson (p, eletric p); Ed Walsh, Bob James (synthesizer); George Benson, Tony Mottola (g); Ray Brown, Gene Cherico, Bob Cranshaw, Marcus Miller, Major Holley (b); Steve Gadd, Irv Cottler (d); Lionel Hampton (vbs); Ralph McDonald (percussion). *NYC, April 13, 16 and 17, 1984*

Oscar Brashear, Gary Grant, Jerry Hey, Snookie Young (tp); George Bohanon, Lew McCreary, Bill Reichenbach, Bill Watrous (tb); Larry Williams, Buddy Collette, William Green, Kim Hutchcroft, Jerome Richardson (reeds); David Duke, Sidney Muldrow, Henry Sigismonti (frh); James Self (tuba); Amy Sherman (harp); Randy Kerber (p, electric p, synthesizer); Craig Huxley (synthesizer); Neil Stubenhaus (b); John Robinson, Ndugu Chancler (d). *LA. May 17, 1984*

Dave Matthews, Jerry Hey, Torri Zito, Joe Parnello, Sam Nestico, Frank Foster (arr); Quincy Jones (arr, producer), Frank Sinatra (vcl).

L.A. IS MY LADY	Qwest (Am) 25145,	(Eu) 925145
THE BEST OF EVERYTHING	"	"
HOW DO YOU KEEP THE MUSIC PLAYING?	"	"
TEACH ME TONIGHT	"	"
IT'S ALL RIGHT WITH ME	"	"
MACK THE KNIFE	"	"
UNTIL THE REAL THING COMES ALONG	"	"
STORMY WEATHER (add Lee Ritenour -g)	"	"
A HUNDRED YEARS FROM TODAY	"	"
IF I SHOULD LOSE YOU	"	"
AFTER YOU'VE GONE	"	"

Title: L.A. is my lady

CHOICE

SEPT '86

Performing Arts

Music

HORRICKS, Raymond. **Quincy Jones,** by Raymond Horricks; selected discography by Tony Middleton. Hippocrene, 1986 (c1985). 127p ill 12.95 ISBN 0-87052-215-9. ML 419. British CIP

Quincy Jones, one of the most successful figures in American music, began his varied career as a performer and composer of jazz (he played and arranged for Count Basie and Lionel Hampton, among others), but before long went on to assume wider-ranging responsibilities. As a top record producer, award-winning film and television composer, musical director for such popular music stars as Michael Jackson, and most recently, film coproducer, Jones has consistently earned praise for his uncompromising artistic standards. Although this slim volume is too brief and unbalanced to constitute a definitive biography—the first 20 highly formative years receive only 5 of the approximately 100 pages of text—it does offer an overview of Jones's career and some insights into his fertile mind. Author of several respected books on jazz and a friend of Jones, Horricks writes about his subject knowledgeably, affectionately, and clearly. The appendix includes film and television credits and a selected discography, but there is no index. Appropriate for all levels, but not essential to a basic undergraduate collection.—*A.D. Franklin, Winthrop College*